EYES OF FAITH

WINNING THE BATTLE BETWEEN
OUR FEELINGS AND OUR FAITH

CAROLYN DALE NEWELL

Published by Carolyn Dale Newell

devotionsforyou@gmail.com

WHAT ARE PEOPLE SAYING ABOUT EYES OF FAITH?

"Carolyn Dale Newell is a true example of 'walking by faith, and not by sight.' Carolyn takes us on a journey of tremendous blessing and reward. It is a journey that is exciting, life-altering, and mind-boggling. It is a journey that will allow you to see and experience God as He was meant to be: in all His fullness and grace. As you read this book, be encouraged to walk by faith—a faith that moves mountains and God's hands."

—Pastor Ray Burton,
New Life Fellowship Church of God of Prophecy

"Are you seeking a new way of looking at life? Then look through the eyes that are hindered to help gain new sight, new insight.

Carolyn Dale Newell writes her beautiful story of coming to faith through the dusty lens of impaired sight. And oh, how she sees!

Here's the deal. You want to see your faith blossom through that same lens. Enjoy reading as your spiritual eyes open."

—Susan B. Mead, award-winning author and radio host of "Find Calm in the Chaos of Life"

"As I read Carolyn's book my soul was refreshed. She speaks candidly of her life experiences and encourages the reader, in her words, to 'make progress in the process.' Her journey of faith is proof that God is still in the miracle business. She gives much insight into how God uses the circumstances in our life to increase our faith and trust in Him. She is living proof that diminished physical sight does not hinder spiritual sight."

—Susie Hamilton, lay minister and author

"Newell's latest release, *Eyes of Faith*, takes readers on a journey of fear-fighting, truth-telling, hope-filling faith. Using personal stories underscored with rich, biblical truths, this book not only encourages readers that they can grow their faith in the midst of difficult circumstances, it also guides them through practical end-of-chapter summary points to help them apply biblical principles to their own lives. In the end, we discover that when our human sight is failing, God is growing something clearer, something stronger—He is growing in us...eyes of faith!"

—Lisa Murray, Licensed Marriage and Family Therapist, author of *Peace for a Lifetime: Embracing a Life of Hope, Wholeness, and Harmony through Emotional Abundance*

"A must-read journey, Carolyn shows us how to see things through Eyes of Faith... A vision that is assisted with the eyes of her black beauty, Iva. Jesus said our eyes are the windows of our heart...with God-inspired guidance and Iva, Carolyn provides us with motivation and direction."

—Cindy Crain, retired editor

"More than one person has taken their disability and used it as a crutch to hobble through this life into the next, but Carolyn has taken her difficulties and used them to be an encouragement to so many who are struggling with theirs. She has taken each one as stepping stones to become the godly, insightful woman she has become! We all need to find our spiritual eyes and find our own divine calling!"

—Tammy Smith, pastor's wife,
Fountain of Life Church of God of Prophecy

Thanks to my husband, Timmy, for his support and assistance with this book. I love you dearly.

Thanks to Pastor Ray, sister Nikki, and my New Life Fellowship family for their prayers, support, love, and encouragement.

CONTENTS

INTRODUCTION

This book took on new life. What begin as my memoir turned into something quite different.

The subject was always faith, but as I began rewriting the entire book, God taught me a valuable lesson about trusting Him. Within our minds, a battle rages on. Our brains are filled with past experiences and learned behaviors. But it is in our minds that we must make important decisions based on the Word of God. We have the power to choose faith over every emotion that exists including fear, doubt, worry, and discouragement.

Today, many people are controlled by their feelings rather than controlling their feelings with their faith. In this book, you will learn to overrule your emotions with an utmost trust in God.

All Scriptures, unless otherwise noted, are from the New King James Version of the Bible.

Scripture taken from the New King James Version. Copyright © 1982 by Thomas Nelson, Inc. Used by permission. All rights reserved.

Edited by Lucie Winborne

Author photo by John Vecchiolla Photography

Formatting and cover design by eBook Launch

Cover photo by Timothy Newell

PART I

LEARNING TO TRUST GOD

Chapter 1

Released

My heart pulsated like a drum. Anticipation raced through my veins. I hadn't experienced this type of excitement since I was a child at Christmas. Enthusiasm had kept me awake most of the night, and now the big moment was here. No wrapping paper or boxes to tear into, just standing on a New York sidewalk waiting on Lori, my trainer.

Lori had played this role many times, and she knew the exhilaration overwhelming her student as she introduced me to a female black Labrador Retriever.

Black Beauty seemed almost as excited as me. Tail wagging, she had a pep in her step. As students at Guiding Eyes for the Blind (GEB), we weren't allowed to know the names of our potential dogs until "dog day," twenty-four hours away. Black Beauty greeted me by taking my hand gently in her mouth. I stroked her head and back as I said hello. Would she be my guide dog? Today was our test drive.

Lori had her support leash attached to my dog. I lifted the harness as Lori instructed me to give the forward command. Off we went, whizzing down the sidewalk. Lori gave commentary as to what we were approaching so I wouldn't be startled by any sudden changes.

First, some metal grids occupied the center of the sidewalk, but my little assistant avoided them by going to the left. Lori explained that the dogs don't want to walk on the metal grids.

As we neared the curb, my guide dog ever so gently came to a halt. We crossed a street while cars on our left hurried to their next destination. This small-town girl wasn't accustomed to such heavy traffic, but my little friend didn't seem to mind.

Now we began winding in and out of people, never bumping into anyone. Impressive. Black Beauty went through the crowd like a hot knife through butter. I hadn't moved at those speeds in years. Not even with my fast-paced husband.

People chattered. Horns honked. The aroma of lunch escaped through an open door. A toddler yelled "Doggie." Wow! My dog wasn't distracted by anything. Lori warned me of an upcoming distraction; pigeons feasting on some delicacy they had discovered. Their wings fluttered as they cooed, but surprisingly, my black beauty ignored the pigeons' festivities.

A breeze momentarily cooled me as we raced to the next curb where again she slowed before hitting the brakes. Then, she curled around me seeking her treat and praise, which I lovingly offered her.

Freedom. Pure freedom. It felt normal to walk with a dog and not my white cane. It triggered memories of how I could walk before my vision became worse. I felt the chains drop off. I had been released from the confines of a disability.

I don't speak for every visually impaired person, but I felt limited by the cane. On these bustling sidewalks of White Plains, New York, I would have poked along with the cane, apologizing to each person it struck.

On my first walk with a guide dog, I envisioned many doors opening with this new mode of travel. No longer did I feel enslaved to the cane. Now, I could walk with the agility I had as a teen or at least a twenty-something. I felt like a caged bird who had found an open door, and yes, we could fly.

The following day, I anxiously awaited the moment I'd learn which dog would be my match. A black female named Iva. I anticipated Iva's arrival in my dorm room. I knew when she greeted me, I recognized her personality as the black beauty I had walked the previous day. Iva, God's precious gift, wrapped in black fur, would forever change my life and the lives of many others. The truth had set me free.

Why did it take so long for me to discover the liberty of walking with a service dog? Myths. *You must work outside the house to obtain a dog. They will remove the dog at any time for any reason. The training requires you to leave home and attend a guide dog school for six months. The cane is more accurate.* None of these myths proved to be true, especially the one about the cane's accuracy.

I recall another walk of independence, over twenty years ago. At the time, I couldn't apprehend the freedom I was embracing. Once again, I had to discern between truth and error.

On that particular day, I anxiously left the house, determined to head to the altar. Not one more troubling day could pass without salvation. The cold March morning air stung my cheeks. Every step I took resulted in a sharp pinch on my toes. The discomfort intensified as the steep hill descended toward the church.

My seven-year-old daughter complained about her tiny feet hurting. Sneakers may have been a better choice for her. I was meeting God, not trying to win a fashion contest. We both wore cheap black dress shoes. Easy on the pocketbook, but hard on the feet.

Was the church really this far away? Maybe it should break the record for the longest walk to an altar in history.

Hoping to soothe my sweet daughter's complaints, and my silent ones, I told her we would never have to walk this way again. We had grown accustomed to walking, since her father and I had divorced several years earlier. I never had a driver's license due to my visual impairment, but transportation to and from church has never been an issue since that day. God has provided.

We passed one church, and I momentarily considered stopping. Warm hands and relief for our weary feet beckoned to me. No, I wanted the church I called with the friendly man on the other end of the phone. He cheerfully gave me their schedule, and something in his voice sounded inviting.

As I opened the church door that long-ago March morning, I started to feel relieved. Not a minute too soon for our sore feet, but the cleansing of my tainted soul brought the greatest relief. Friendly faces greeted us as we entered the sanctuary. Warmth filled my heart as well as my shivering body. A kind lady escorted my daughter to children's church.

I took a seat in a comfortable pew. I waited for the altar call. My childhood church did not have altar calls, but I had seen one when I had visited another church.

I slipped out of my seat and approached the white-haired preacher, Pastor Art. I recognized his friendly voice as the man who spoke to me on the phone a few days earlier. As soon as I reached him, I blurted out my need for redemption. I didn't even know if I should bow down on my knees. I just knew I needed Jesus.

Pastor Art prayed. I prayed. He presented me to the church as a newborn Christian. Shouts of "Amen" filled the church, unlike my usual church experiences. Everyone came by and gave me hugs.

Perhaps you remember the day God saved you. Maybe you don't recall the date, but you know without a doubt Jesus Christ is your personal Savior. Even though I never tasted saving faith until age thirty-three, I cherish fond childhood memories of Sunday School and Vacation Bible School. I can still sing the songs we learned. Fun songs with serious messages. Have you ever heard this one?

"The wise man built his house upon the rock…
And the rain came tumbling down
Oh, the rain came down
And the floods came up…
And the wise man's house stood firm.
The foolish man built his house upon the sand…
And the rain came tumbling down
Oh, the rain came down
And the floods came up…
And the foolish man's house went splat!"*

The foolish man's house couldn't withstand the storm because its foundation was faulty. But it is not just a silly song for children to sing. It came from the lips of Jesus Christ:

"Therefore whoever hears these sayings of Mine, and does them, I will liken him to a wise man who built his house on the rock: and the rain descended, the floods came, and the winds blew and beat on that house; and it did not fall, for it was founded on the rock. But everyone who hears these sayings of Mine, and does not do them, will be like a foolish man who built his house on the sand: and the rain descended, the floods came, and the winds blew and beat on that house; and it fell. And great was its fall." (Matthew 7:24-27)

Like the myths about guide dogs, this foolish man had built his house on...well, let's call them what they are...lies. Satan is not anti-religious. If he can delude groups of people into a false sense of salvation (and he does), he can keep many souls from God's truth and blessings. Our house cannot be constructed on a fraudulent foundation, or the result will be like the foolish man's house on the sand. We must build on the only truth, the rock. Our Rock, Jesus Christ.

Before God saved me, I genuinely struggled to understand the truth about salvation. I talked to everyone I thought might have a clue about religion. I heard all sorts of lies.

Salvation comes through water baptism. Lie! *Salvation occurs when you join the church.* Lie! *You earn your salvation by the good works you do.* Another lie!

Deceived people deceive people.

Do you know what I remember along with the multiple definitions of salvation I received? No one showed me the Bible. No one quoted Scripture. I didn't know any better then, but I do now.

Sharing the gospel is difficult, but I would never do it without Scripture. I don't want people to take my word for it. I want them to hear it from the lips of God, from His living, breathing Word.

Do you ever find yourself wandering if your salvation is real, or do you fumble over the words to use when you witness to others? If so, this chapter will help you discern between the fake and the only truth that sets us free. The truth of Jesus Christ.

"Nor is there salvation in any other, for there is no other name under heaven given among men by which we must be saved." (Acts 4:12)

Friend, I have learned the truth, and I found it helps us to become familiar with the passages of the Bible that teach salvation, so we can share it with others. Salvation is the starting point for our faith. Are you ready to dive into Scripture?

My preacher friend, Mike, has a unique approach to witnessing. First, we have to reveal the person's lost condition. Otherwise, they won't realize they need the cure for their sickness. Sin sickness.

This technique doesn't hone in on their most heinous sin, such as fornication or drunkenness. We tell them about the sins we all are guilty of: lying, stealing, and hatred. If we begin with their most horrible sin, we have already made them defensive.

Mike starts with this question: Are you a good person? The typical response is, "Yes. I pay my taxes, keep my lawn clean, give to charity, and I attend church. Yes, I am a good person."

Mike's next questions are as follows: Have you ever lied? Have you ever stolen anything, even as a child? Have you ever hated someone or lusted after a man or a woman?

Even if we were talking to King David, a man after God's own heart (Acts 13:22), his answers would be yes. King David was guilty on all counts, and so are we.

Lying and stealing are prohibited in the Ten Commandments. According to Jesus Christ, lust is equal to committing adultery (Matthew 5:27-28), and hatred is synonymous with murder (Matthew 5:21-22). Now our good person is a lying, thieving, adulterous murderer, just like David.

There is none who does good, no, not one. (Romans 3:12b)

for all have sinned and fall short of the glory of God (Romans 3:23)

For the wages of sin is *death, but the gift of God* is *eternal life in Christ Jesus our Lord.* (Romans 6:23)

We are all sinners. We all must die, but Jesus Christ, the sinless Son of God, died for us. His never-ending love runs so deep that He went to the cross to pay, to make atonement, for our sins.

Now, let's see what the greatest Preacher, Jesus Christ, says about salvation.

In John chapter three, Nicodemus, a ruler of the Jews, came to see Jesus, under the cover of darkness. The Pharisees weren't fans of Christ, and Nicodemus probably did not want his fellow Pharisees to know he went seeking answers from Jesus.

Jesus knows the hearts and minds of all people, so He answered Nicodemus' question before he could utter the words.

Jesus answered and said to him, "Most assuredly, I say to you, unless one is born again, he cannot see the kingdom of God." (John 3:3)

I love this verse, because Jesus tells us how to get to heaven, the kingdom of God. I wish someone had shared it with me when I was seeking the truth.

Since the only way to enter God's kingdom is to be born again, literally "born from above," it rules out all the wrong roads to heaven.

The wrong road to heaven is the right road to hell.

Did we have anything to do with our first birth? No, and we have nothing to do with our second birth either.

We didn't perform good works to be physically born, and good works have nothing to do with our second birth either.

Salvation doesn't occur because of good works. Good works occur because of salvation.

Good works are evidence of salvation. The same is true for church membership. It should take place after salvation, not as a means of obtaining eternal life. We must be born again!

Nicodemus with all his intellect couldn't grasp this concept. The Jews thought they would automatically be ushered into the kingdom of God because of their nationality, being descendants of Abraham. Jesus rocked Nicodemus' theology. With all his knowledge, he didn't know God. He only knew about Him.

Jesus answered, "Most assuredly, I say to you, unless one is born of water and the Spirit, he cannot enter the kingdom of God." (John 3:5)

Jesus reiterated His point. You must be born of the Spirit, Nick, not your Jewish heritage and not your synagogue attendance or prominence in society. The notes on this verse in the Life Application study Bible say that the Kingdom is personal, not political or ethnical, and that entrance requirements are repentance and spiritual rebirth.

I haven't found a study Bible or commentator that says without a doubt what it means to be born of water. One thing they all agree on is that it doesn't refer to water baptism.

Most likely, it points to the cleansing power of the Word of God and the sanctifying work of the Holy Spirit.

not by works of righteousness which we have done, but according to His mercy He saved us, through the washing of regeneration and renewing of the Holy Spirit, (Titus 3:5)

Here, we are reminded that salvation is not of works. Titus uses the theological term "regeneration," which refers to the new birth.

Next, Jesus gave Nicodemus an earthly analogy.

"Do not marvel that I said to you, 'You must be born again.' The wind blows where it wishes, and you hear the sound of it, but cannot tell where it comes from and where it goes. So is everyone who is born of the Spirit." (John 3:7-8)

Tree branches scattered about, patio chairs overturned, and power lines down were proof that the high winds had come through our neighborhood. We never saw the wind. We heard it, but until we viewed the effects of it, we could not realize its power. Humans cannot control the wind. They struggle to give timely warnings about devastating tornadoes that rip through towns leaving a path of destruction as proof of their existence.

Likewise, we cannot see the Spirit, but we can observe the Spirit's effect on a renewed life. The drunk who doesn't return to the bottle. The dirty mouth of a sinner made clean by the Holy Spirit. That is the evidence of the Spirit, and like the wind, humans are not in control.

The need to be in charge of our lives is a substantial hurdle to salvation. We want to be proud. We want to say, "Look at what I did! Look how I cleaned up. I am a reformed jerk!" The transformed saint declares, "Look what God did with a sinner such as I."

Poor Nicodemus still couldn't get it, and Jesus lovingly chided him. Nicodemus, you're a renowned teacher, how come you still don't understand? So, Jesus used an Old Testament type of His crucifixion. Nicodemus knew the Old Testament well.

And as Moses lifted up the serpent in the wilderness, even so must the Son of Man be lifted up, (John 3:14)

In Numbers chapter 21, the Lord sent fiery serpents because the discouraged Israelites complained about their circumstances. They even grumbled about the manna God had bountifully provided them. Many Israelites were bitten and died, so those remaining confessed their sins. Instead of removing the serpents, the Lord instructed Moses to construct a bronze serpent on a pole. When a serpent bit someone, they could look at the bronze serpent and they would live.

Likewise, God hasn't removed sin from the world, but when we are bitten by sin, we can look to Jesus Christ and receive forgiveness.

For God so loved the world that He gave His only begotten Son, that whoever believes in Him should not perish but have everlasting life. (John 3:16)

This memorable verse is the gospel in a nutshell. "For God so loved." John used the word "so" because no word rightly describes the depth of God's love. It is an unconditional love we cannot fathom. No human loves like that. We exhaust ourselves trying to hang on to an earthly love that was never designed to appease our craving for compassion. Our insatiable appetite for love is only satisfied by Jesus.

Christ love is exalting, not exhausting.

We don't need to jump through hoops to gain the love of our Lord. He loved us when we were unlovable, shameful, and sinful.

But God demonstrates His own love toward us, in that while we were still sinners, Christ died for us. (Romans 5:8)

Prior to salvation, I believed in God and Jesus Christ, just like I believed in George Washington and Abraham Lincoln.

Many churches teach easy-believism, and that was what I possessed, not genuine salvation. Repentance and an old-fashioned altar call have been replaced by signing a church membership card. As long as you "believe," you have a fire insurance plan to prevent you from scorching in hell. There is one problem: it is a lie from the father of all lies.

The word "believe" in John 3:16 does not mean we believe Jesus existed. Biblically speaking, believing has the connotation of trusting. When we trust Jesus as Savior and Lord, He saves us. He births us into the family.

It also means we trust Him as Lord of our lives. Master of our lives. Some folks shy away from that one, but how can you give your life to Christ without surrendering your life completely to Him?

The devil and his demons also believed the way I did in those early years (James 2:19). Our enemy, the father of lies, is a sly trickster. He specializes in making lies appear as truth. Sadly, his schemes fool many people, even some preachers.

And Nicodemus was one of them. The Jews believed they were the only race that would inherit the kingdom of God, but when Jesus told Nick God loved the entire world, Nick's world just got rocked again. Let's not be too hard on Nicodemus. Satan has blinded millions. All false religions trust in the works of man, not the work of God. That is the difference between Christianity and the world's religions, but sadly, within the realm of Christianity, people still trust in something they have done.

Everlasting life and eternal life are one and the same. Genuine believers will not see death. Their physical bodies will pass from this world, but their souls will be present with the Lord to live forever. Unbelievers will spend eternity in hell, burning in the fire that never goes out.

Eternal life is not a quantity of life, it is also a quality of life. No, life will not be trouble free. Actually, Christians often suffer more in this world than unbelievers. However, there will come a time when we will never shed another tear. We will never feel heartache. We will never suffer loss and pain.

Jesus said:

"The thief does not come except to steal, and to kill, and to destroy. I have come that they may have life, and that they may have it more abundantly." (John 10:10)

Abundant life begins here. We don't wait until we reach the city limits of heaven to enjoy it. As children of God, we bear the fruit of the Spirit. We experience joy inexpressible. Peace guards our hearts and minds. God strengthens us so we can accomplish whatever tasks He sets before us. Limitless grace is available for the asking.

Christians know God, as well as knowing about Him. God who heals. God who provides. God who comforts. We know Him!

Jesus concludes His conversation with Nicodemus.

"He who believes in Him is not condemned; but he who does not believe is condemned already, because he has not believed in the name of the only begotten Son of God." (John 3:18)

Again, "believe" means "to trust." When Adam sinned, all humanity fell into condemnation. As Adam's descendants, we are already hell-bound, but those who trust in Jesus Christ as their Lord and Savior will never face condemnation, Still, people refuse to place their trust in Christ. They won't relinquish the reins of their life.

"And this is the condemnation, that the light has come into the world, and men loved darkness rather than light, because their deeds were evil. For everyone practicing evil hates the light and does not come to the light, lest his deeds should be exposed. But he who does the truth comes to the light, that his deeds may be clearly seen, that they have been done in God." (John 3:19-21)

A true saint is drawn to the light, Jesus Christ, the light of the world. But the unregenerate love their sin, they don't want the light to expose their evil deeds.

Deep in sin, I would have braved the flames of hell for one more drink. Thankfully, the Lord saved me, and now I drink of the living water, never to thirst again. God saved me from the bondage of sin. I'm not perfect. None of us are, but believers strive for holiness.

Christians are free from sin, not free to sin.

The Spirit demonstrates evidence of His work in our lives. We cherish time with God, in prayer and in His Word. We anticipate Sunday morning to fellowship with believers and feast upon heavenly manna. We are changed, transformed forever.

I live for Jesus because Jesus lives in me.

Several years ago, I gained an appreciation for the freedom Jesus has given me. Drums pounded. Instruments blended harmoniously, as the lyrics about freedom echoed. Every song the Gaither Vocal Band sang directly or indirectly pointed towards freedom.

Many years earlier, I had sat in the same civic center for a rock concert. I reflected momentarily on the drunken state I was in then. I shouted out a praise of thanks. God had rescued me from a life of slavery. Now I was His child. That is the evidence of where the Spirit has been, just like the analogy about the wind Jesus used.

Nick tasted that same freedom. A closet Christian, until the death of Jesus, Nicodemus helped prepare the body for burial (John 19:39).

Dear friend, I don't know your struggles, but I do know if you sincerely seek God, He will lead you into the truth. If you have any doubts about your salvation, please settle it now. I want to meet you on those golden streets one day.

You are not promised tomorrow. We never know what changes a day can bring. Today can be your day of salvation. Prayerfully read John chapter three.

Jesus will return to this earth soon. We must be ready. Are you confident you have a personal relationship with Jesus Christ?

Let's share this life-saving gospel with others. The Lord will qualify us to witness. We can take our Bibles, showing them the gospel of John. Imagine the impact we will have on the lost world when we each share with one person!

The truth that set us free will set the captives free. I am excited we are taking this journey together. We have a long trip ahead, and genuine salvation is the prerequisite. Faith frees…in so many ways, as you will soon see.

Lord Jesus, reveal Your truth to my friend. Let them know they belong to You. Help us to share the gospel with others. In Jesus' name, Amen.

Stepping Stones

Deceived people deceive people.

The wrong road to heaven is the right road to hell.

Salvation doesn't occur because of good works. Good works occur because of salvation.

Christ love is exalting, not exhausting.

Christians are free from sin, not free to sin.

I live for Jesus because Jesus lives in me.

Scripture

There is none who does good, no, not one. (Romans 3:12b)

for all have sinned and fall short of the glory of God (Romans 3:23)

For the wages of sin is death, but the gift of God is eternal life in Christ Jesus our Lord. (Romans 6:23)

Jesus answered and said to him, "Most assuredly, I say to you, unless one is born again, he cannot see the kingdom of God." (John 3:3)

Jesus answered, "Most assuredly, I say to you, unless one is born of water and the Spirit, he cannot enter the kingdom of God." (John 3:5)

"Do not marvel that I said to you, 'You must be born again.' The wind blows where it wishes, and you hear the sound of it, but cannot tell where it comes from and where it goes. So is everyone who is born of the Spirit." (John 3:7-8)

For God so loved the world that He gave His only begotten Son, that whoever believes in Him should not perish but have everlasting life. (John 3:16)

But God demonstrates His own love toward us, in that while we were still sinners, Christ died for us. (Romans 5:8)

The thief does not come except to steal, and to kill, and to destroy. I have come that they may have life, and that they may have it more abundantly. (John 10:10)

"He who believes in Him is not condemned; but he who does not believe is condemned already, because he has not believed in the name of the only begotten Son of God." (John 3:18)

- http://childbiblesongs.com/song-21-wise-man-built-his-house.shtml

CHAPTER 2

LIVING LOVED

We live in a world permeated with trouble, and sometimes our trials confuse us. We can't perceive why God allows horrific things in our lives. We become discouraged. We become disappointed in God. Even angry at Him. Then we wonder ... does God still love me?

If God genuinely loves me, why is this happening? The child loses the battle with cancer. The accident that turned your world upside down. The husband God took too early from you. The healing that never came. The prodigal who never returned home.

"Naked I came from my mother's womb,
And naked shall I return there.
The Lord gave, and the Lord has taken away;
Blessed be the name of the Lord." (Job 1:21)

I discovered I knew little about God's love for us. Since my salvation, I had buried myself deep in Bible study for twenty-two years. I had studied even more during my six years in ministry, but I hadn't grasped the concept of His love.

We fail to understand God's unfailing love.

Last spring, Pastor Ray asked me to deliver the Mother's Day message. I almost declined, feeling unworthy. My daughter wasn't a Christian. She is a homosexual, but my pastor knew that. She had left home at age eighteen, and for eight years, I never heard from her. I was not the one who should give the Mother's Day message. Shame settled upon me as I recalled my shortcomings as a mom.

Then my mind went to my fingertips. What was I working on? I was writing about mommas who hurt. I thought about all the

Mother's Days when I avoided church. Avoided the pain, or so I thought. Many women had shared their heartache with me. Yes, I will do it because this message will comfort those women. Women who had never conceived. Women who had miscarried or buried their children. And women like me with a wayward child. Even those moms with a homosexual son or daughter.

While I prepared that message, I found it was as much for me as it was for any momma. God showed me the true reason I never attended church on Mother's Day. The devil had shamed me. He made me feel unworthy, like a failure as a mom. I was ashamed to stand with the other moms. So, I stayed home almost every year.

As Mother's Day 2018 drew near, I became nervous. This would be my first message to the entire church, not just the women. This would also be the first time I delivered a message before Pastor Ray.

"I hope Pastor Ray is pleased with my message." I repeated it several times.

"Why are you worried about what a man thinks?" asked my husband.

Ouch! He had a point, but I blurted out my concern for Pastor Ray's approval. My ministry had lacked support from my previous pastors. Now I was at a new church. A new denomination. And I was shepherded by an extremely encouraging pastor.

"As long as God is pleased, it shouldn't matter what anyone else thinks."

I hate it when my husband is right. But he had revealed that my focus was misplaced. God's stamp of approval is the only one we need, not just in ministry but concerning our entire Christian life. If we seek the acceptance of others, we are doing it for the wrong reasons.

So, my summer to learn about God's acceptance and love began. Rejection played an important role in my life from an early age. I had good parents. No abuse like many children endure. My parents weren't the affectionate type. I always loved when our out-of-town relatives visited because they were full of hugs.

As a child with a visual impairment, you can imagine the teasing that took place at school. Gym class was a nightmare. Not only did I end up being the last person chosen to be on a team, but the two team captains bickered back and forth about who got stuck with me.

When I was about fourteen, I bought a T-shirt that read, "Hug me, I'm lonely." I was starving for acceptance, especially from my peers. And even more importantly, from a boy.

At age seventeen, I found what I had been seeking in the party crowd. Their acceptance encouraged me to join them. That became my way of life until I met someone who stuck around long enough to get married. I left the party life behind to have my only child. Someone I loved and who would love me. Then I was divorced.

God saved me a few years later, but I never grasped how much He loved me. As a Christian, I still placed a high value on the acceptance of others, because I never viewed myself as an accepted and beloved child of God.

I married a second time. My husband loved me dearly. I made new friends in church after God saved me, but the rejection of my daughter must have stirred up feelings of being unwanted again.

Sometimes I felt like it was me and Jesus against the world. Nobody but Christ could empathize with my broken heart. Not even my husband. Feeling the presence of Jesus isn't always equal to sensing His immeasurable love.

After my first book, *In the Storm*, released, I prepared myself concerning sales. Overlook the first twenty to thirty sales. They would come from friends and church members. Real interest would show up afterward.

My hopes plummeted when sales stopped at five. I was spreading encouragement. Shouldn't people want to support me with a one-dollar book?

That's when approval seeking became a priority once again. It became clear that most preachers aren't interested in a testimony about overcoming a disability. Not enough to invite a woman to share her story in their church. Not everyone loves you just because you are in ministry. Like everywhere else in life, haters hang out there too.

I became keenly aware of the numerous times I was excluded. Anything from being left alone in a room to being left out altogether. Every rejection built up, layer upon layer. All along, God loved me immensely, but I focused on the cliques I wasn't part of.

Eventually, I left my church of twenty-two years to serve in a women's ministry at another church. Pastor Ray eagerly supported my book in progress, my ministry, and me.

"Go where you are celebrated, not tolerated." - Kathy Crabb Hannah

I soon ascertained God had brought me to New Life Fellowship for something more than ministry. These people loved me, and they all loved Iva too. When I joined the church, they made Iva an honorary member. Finally, I was surrounded with men and women alike who supported me.

But now, God lifted up my chin and spoke right to my heart. *I love you more. I accept you more. I am the one who made you acceptable.*

We sit in church every week, and we are told God loves us. We read in our Bibles about God's love. A precious treasure has become too familiar to us. Like the constant drip, drip, drip of a leaky faucet, we get accustomed to it, and the truth loses its value.

God's magnificent love doesn't mean as much to us as it did on the day He saved us. We speed across those verses to get to the meatier ones. You know, the ones we need today that tell us God will help us. God will strengthen us. God will provide for us. But if we stopped and meditated on the love God has for us, we would already know He is going to do everything to take care of His precious children.

The enemy of our souls doesn't want us to feel loved by God. Complacency is just one way he carries out that task. But it isn't the only one.

You might be one of the many people who have bad memories of your earthly father. You never knew him. He deserted you. He hurt you. He abused you. Now, you have a real struggle with God the Father. You have a relationship with Jesus Christ, but you cannot relate to a father figure.

Has a wretched past caused you to believe you are unacceptable to God? *God doesn't love me, not like He loves others. I will never please Him. I'll never be good enough.*

If you can relate to any of the above, you must learn something about God's love. Truthfully, we all need to hear this, because God's love is unfathomable. Before we can try to overcome fear, discouragement, and worry by trusting God completely, we need to appreciate the depths of God's love.

We assume all love is equal, but God's love cannot compare with any other type of love. It is as different as light and darkness. As different as dark sodas and the lemon-lime varieties.

In 1967, the soft drink 7UP was given a new nickname, the Uncola, an appropriate name because 7UP isn't really a cola.

We are about to see how God's love is the Unlove. His love is so unlike human love and everything that defines love that it actually should have a different name. I found seven "un" words that will aid us in trying to understand the unfathomable love of God. And that was our first word, unfathomable.

We will never understand the love of God, but we must strive to obtain a better comprehension of it. Sadly, our familiarity with the topic creates somewhat of a barrier. We think we know everything, and we spend little time digging into the vastness of divine love.

God's love is unconditional. While we were ungodly, while we were sinners, God loved us (Romans 5:8). God created us in His image (Genesis 1:27). He knows how we feel. He knows our thoughts. He is the expert on what makes us tick.

God is an emotional being. He gave us our emotions: anger, happiness, frustration, love, and sadness. The problem is our emotions are sin-tainted. They lie to us, but God knows that better than we do.

God's love is undeserving. God chose to love us. It wasn't based on anything we did, but He chose to set His affection on us. And He did it before the foundation of the world (Ephesians 1:4). He adopted us as joint heirs with Christ (Ephesians 1:5), and He made us accepted in the Beloved (Ephesians 1:6).

Notice God made us accepted. His love ran so deep He designed a brilliant plan to redeem us.

We fail to understand God's unfailing love.

God's love is unfailing.

The Lord has appeared of old to me, saying:
"Yes, I have loved you with an everlasting love;
Therefore with lovingkindness I have drawn you." (Jeremiah 31:3)

God will never stop loving us, no matter what. His love is everlasting. Everlasting never had a time when it began. Therefore, everlasting will never end.

We can't make God not love us.

God's love is unselfish. Human love is selfish. What can someone do for us? If they never do anything, we conclude they don't love us. Not so with God.

God's love is uncompromising. God is love. If God could bleed, He would bleed love. He cannot help but love.

Of course, love doesn't interfere with God's other attributes. He remains holy and just. He still judges between the righteous and unrighteous.

God's love is unparalleled. We see God's love in Jesus Christ. God sent His Son to die in our place. Has anyone else died for you?

But Jesus Christ went to the cross and bore sin's penalty so we can have everlasting life.

No other love comes close to God's love. None other is capable of sharing that type of affection.

We must begin to completely believe God loves us more than any other love we have ever experienced. Not even the best earthly father comes close to God.

God is the Father unlike all other fathers.

I said we need a word other than love to describe God's love. According to *Vine's Expository Dictionary*, the Greek noun is "agape" and the Greek verb is "agapao." These words translated "love" in our Bibles describe the love God has for humanity. It is not an affectionate feeling. It is a choice, exhibited through actions, not emotions.

Agape, the noun, sacrifices, provides, and comforts. It generously gives the peace and grace found nowhere else.

God's love shines brightest in the night.

At first, we may feel as if God has abandoned us. As we travel through the valley, we will embrace the magnitude of our Father's love more greatly than ever before. How can a loving God allow the situations that hurt us?

God doesn't send trials to hurt us, but to help us.

God doesn't allow trouble to harm but to heal. In the midst of my failing vision, I couldn't perceive how God was going to work things together for my good or His glory, but He did. If He had shown me what He was up to, I would have run screaming. God gave me situations where I experienced His grace, to the extent that I wanted to share those experiences through writing.

What we find in the midst of the hurting, the helping, and the healing is the hope. At least once in our lifetime, most of us will encounter a darkness so black that the only hope is God's love. God loves you, and God loves me.

Let's turn to God's Word to get a glance at two sisters who were quite disappointed in Jesus. In John chapter eleven, we have the story about the death and resurrection of Lazarus. The sisters of Lazarus, Mary and Martha, had sent word to Jesus that their brother, Lazarus, was deathly ill. Of course, Jesus knew that.

They didn't need to ask Jesus to heal their brother. Jesus was their close friend. Surely, Jesus would heal Him with a word. They knew about the blind who could see. They knew about the deaf who could hear. They knew about the crippled who could walk. Surely, Jesus would heal His dear friend, Lazarus.

But Jesus didn't heal him. Jesus said the sickness was not unto death, and it would bring God glory. None of that made sense when Lazarus died. The illness that wasn't unto death resulted in the death of Lazarus. Why had Jesus let them down? Why did Jesus promise it would not end in death? Why couldn't they count on Jesus?

Maybe we've asked these same questions before. We might not demand the answers from God, but our thoughts wander.

To make things worse, Jesus delayed going to visit Mary and Martha for two days. His disciples couldn't figure this one out. Their minds must have been racing with questions. Jesus needs to heal Lazarus, but why is He delaying? Doesn't Jesus love Lazarus? What if it were one of us? Can we count on Jesus?

Even today, as we read this passage, we might wonder why Jesus waited so long. Why did He cause their grief to drag on when He had something wonderful planned? Why did He let Mary and Martha suffer?

These verses are packed with biblical truths, but let's only concentrate on the love of Jesus.

When sorrow occurs, Jesus still loves us. When we are confused, Jesus still loves us.

Circumstances aren't the thermometers by which we measure God's love.

Bad things happen, even to believers. Why? Sin entered this world, and through sin, death also entered. Along with sin and death came hatred, crimes, disease, and abuse.

When we are heartbroken, Jesus' plan proceeds on His timetable. He doesn't intend to drag out the sadness, but He has a perfect plan. One we must trust.

Lazarus had to remain in that grave several days to demonstrate the glory of the Lord. Jesus had raised others from the dead, but no one had ever been resurrected after rigor mortis had set in. No one could deny this miracle.

Sweet friend, remember: when Jesus delays, it isn't a denial.

Mary and Martha's story demonstrates this truth, but can you recall a season in your life when Jesus took His time? Sometimes, it seems like He isn't working at all.

I had yearned so long for speaking engagements, as they slowly trickled in. God had called me to speak. I knew that beyond a shadow of a doubt, but where were the invitations? By the way, patience is not something I do well.

During the waiting, I felt I should invest in my calling. If I don't invest in myself, how can I expect others to invest in me? I had done this with writing, but not speaking, so I paid an exorbitant amount of money to work with speaking coach Amy Carroll.

It was worth every penny. I learned how to write effective messages that also benefitted my writing too. Before I finished working with Amy, I had booked two speaking engagements. One was at our local senior center, and they continue to invite me back.

One night, my husband and I went to the grocery store at an unusually late hour for us. Pastor Ray, who wasn't my pastor at that point, was working the night shift, stocking shelves. We talked for a few minutes, and I shared that I had just completed working with Amy. A few weeks later, Sister Nikki, Pastor Ray's wife, invited me to speak at their ladies' conference.

God works while we wait.

We think we are going nowhere, as if we're stuck in traffic, but God is working behind the scenes. Not only did I get bookings, God led me to a new church.

God sees from above while we only see what's ahead.

When things don't go our way, it has nothing to do with God's love. It has everything to do with God's plan. Our desire should always be God's will, no matter what. God is sovereign, and He sees the whole picture, while we only see one small part.

Someone might ask about the friendship between this family and Jesus. After all, He frequented their home. Martha had cooked for Him, and Mary had anointed Jesus with her expensive perfume. Doesn't that count for anything?

Threads of love run through this story, but they wouldn't exist if Jesus had shown partiality toward Mary and Martha. Do we really want favoritism from Jesus? What if we weren't His special friends?

God is impartial. God loves us all the same. And we can all shout hallelujah now.

When Martha heard Jesus was coming (John 11:20), she hurried to meet Him.

Now Martha said to Jesus, "Lord, if You had been here, my brother would not have died." (John 11:21)

Martha didn't hide her disappointment in Jesus. She boldly expressed her thoughts. My brother could be alive right now, but You did nothing to help.

Then, Martha told Jesus she still trusted Him. She had no hope for her brother, but she didn't lose faith.

"But even now I know that whatever You ask of God, God will give You." (John 11:22)

Martha never lost her faith in Christ. Even after He let her down, her faith remained steadfast. Martha is our example when we can't figure out our situations. Jesus, this doesn't make any sense, but I trust You. We choose to trust, even in the face of disappointment and anger. We must make a conscious decision to continue trusting the Lord. In times when trusting is difficult, we must commit to choose faith.

Next, Mary found Jesus and repeated her sister's words. Brokenhearted and discouraged, Mary allowed Jesus to see her genuine feelings. Perhaps these sisters knew they could hide nothing from Jesus. We must admire their honesty.

How many times do we pray as usual when deep down we hold on to our anger, pain, and guilt? Why can't we have the same openness as Martha and Mary?

At the sight of Mary's tears, Jesus groaned within Himself and was troubled (John 11:33).

This verse should give us great comfort. God has compassion for His children. It grieves the Lord to see us sorrow because He sees the effects of sin on His beloved.

He is moved by our tears. He collects them in a bottle and records them in His book (Psalm 56:8). One day, He will wipe our tears away (Revelation 7:17).

Mary and Martha's story ends with the unique miraculous resurrection of Lazarus. Four days in the grave. Many songs have been written to explain that Jesus wasn't four days late, but He was right on time. The Bible tells us that many people wanted to hear Lazarus tell his story. It would be interesting to know what he experienced, but I want to hear another story. The one about the love and comfort received from Jesus while they thought their brother was dead.

God's light shines brightest in the night.

And it was during their blackest of nights that they felt the loving arms of Jesus. Jesus wasn't with them, but God the Father reached down to comfort and help these sisters. That's the story I want to hear.

Martha continued to trust Jesus in the midst of a terrible situation because she felt the touch of God. His grace. His strength. We can't feel His comfort until we cry. We can't feel His strength until we are weak. We can't feel His grace until we are needy. We don't like the dark seasons of our lives, but we will never see the love of God shine any brighter until we pass through those dark valleys.

My friend, you may be there right now. Perhaps it is the darkest time of your life. Whatever you are going through today, know that God loves you. You are safe in His love, the most secure place for a Christian.

We have the confidence that no matter how horrible things get, we are still loved by God. No matter what we do, we are still loved by God. The world can hate us. They hated Jesus, but we are still loved by God. The devil and his demons can fight us, but they can never separate us from the love of God (Romans 8:38-39).

My Mother's Day message was greatly received as was the lesson I learned from my heavenly Father. I had victory on a day that had produced grievous pain for many years. No longer would I feel ashamed as a mom.

And now, I live loved. I take time to rejoice in that great love of God. Will you join me?

Take a few moments every now and then to meditate on God's love. If we do that daily, I fear it might become redundant, but maybe a couple times a week, during our quiet time, we can intentionally concentrate on God's tender lovingkindness.

It will serve as a reminder of how special His love is, and how special we are to be loved by Him. We need to know our worth to Him. When we absorb that truth, we can live loved.

What will that look like? Days of complaining will transpire into days of rejoicing. Who can grumble when they dig into the depths of God's love?

Times of disappointment and discouragement will evaporate. Our trust in the God who loves us supremely will increase. We will draw near to God, and He will draw nearer to us (James 4:8).

When we make a point to reflect on the magnificent love of our Lord, we will linger in prayer and worship. Joy will flood our hearts because we know we are loved by our supreme God.

I'm not suggesting we will never have another bad day. Far from it.

God's love shines brightest in the night.

My prayer is that now your knowledge about God's love has grown. That is vital for the remainder of this book. If you doubt God's love, how can your faith increase? How can we move forward to a deeper trust in Him?

Before you can eradicate fear, doubt, and worry, you must try to understand this unfathomable love as much as possible. You must know the God you are placing your trust in. Otherwise, it is going to be difficult to wholeheartedly trust God when you don't acknowledge His love.

I don't know why God would choose to value and love me, but I am overjoyed that He does. I certainly don't deserve it. He deserves better than I can give. How can I not commune with Him at length? How can I not remind myself that I am the accepted, beloved, and chosen daughter of the King? And so are you, sweet friend.

We will experience more of His abundant life. That takes us from living loved to loving life. Life can be rich and full when we win the battle between our feelings and our faith.

Heavenly Father, You truly are a good, good Father. How blessed we are to know You and call You our Daddy. Lord, help us feel Your mighty arms wrap around us as we take this journey of faith. In Jesus' name, Amen.

Stepping Stones

We fail to understand God's unfailing love.

We can't make God not love us.

God is the Father unlike all other fathers.

God's love shines brightest in the night.

God doesn't send trials to hurt us, but to help us.

Circumstances aren't the thermometers by which we measure God's love.

When Jesus delays, it isn't a denial.

God works while we wait.

God sees from above while we only see what's ahead.

"Naked I came from my mother's womb,
And naked shall I return there.
The Lord gave, and the Lord has taken away;
Blessed be the name of the Lord." (Job 1:21)
The Lord has appeared of old to me, saying:
"Yes, I have loved you with an everlasting love;
Therefore with lovingkindness I have drawn you." (Jeremiah 31:3)

CHAPTER 3

PROGRESS IN THE PROCESS

Timmy, my hubby-to-be, crouched on the floor, facing me. I squirmed on the edge of the sofa. This wasn't going to be good. I could feel it already. His serious tone alerted me that something was very wrong.

"The doctor says I have leukemia."

Leukemia. I didn't even know how to spell it, but at the sound of the word, the floodgate opened to a river of tears. Timmy tried reassuring me, explaining that a bone marrow transplant could save his life. Transplants are invasive, and at the mention of that word, my heart sank even deeper. On that spring day, I had no clue how invasive they could really be.

"No, no…" I uttered between sobs.

This could not be happening. We weren't even married yet! This should be our season for beginnings, not disease and death. As God's creation began anew with leaves budding on the trees. Flowers sprang up from their winter nap. Birds celebrated life as they sang. Winter was over, but not for us.

One glimmer of hope shone through the darkness. The only way to diagnose leukemia was a bone marrow biopsy. Once Timmy had that painful procedure, it took almost two weeks to get the results. During that time, we prayed for another diagnosis. It could be anything, just not cancer.

The official diagnosis came back as chronic myelogenous leukemia (CML). Not what we wanted to hear. I feared losing the love of my life.

Pastor Art directed Timmy to read James 5:14-15:

Is anyone among you sick? Let him call for the elders of the church, and let them pray over him, anointing him with oil in the name of the Lord. And the prayer of faith will save the sick, and the Lord will raise him up.

That evening, the men from our church met for prayer and the anointing. As Pastor Art and another preacher laid hands on Timmy, he felt a strange burning sensation travel from their hands throughout his body. No, it was not an immediate healing. Miracles in progress are plentiful today, but they are still miracles.

An oncologist scheduled Timmy for an appointment with a transplant specialist. We put it off until after our wedding. Meanwhile, Timmy took an oral medication. We believed God would work a miracle through it, but the meds simply controlled his symptoms, like a lid on a pot of boiling water. The water continues to boil, and the CML remained.

We consulted with a transplant specialist who rocked our world. An earthquake could not have shattered us more. Two weeks of wedded bliss, and then the doctor revealed the horrors of life post-transplant. Timmy would have to stay surrounded by a plastic tent with no physical contact. Not a touch. Not a kiss. The tent would protect him from infection since chemo and radiation would destroy his blood cells. All cells, good and cancerous. Then they would introduce the new bone marrow, hoping it would flourish and his body would not view it as a foreign invader.

Among all the frightening things we learned that day, I remember the plastic tent most. The human touch soothes and comforts. How could my touch be harmful?

Our beautiful world, as we knew it, would change drastically. Even worse, it could cease to exist.

Timmy chose not to have this drastic procedure. OK, he would not have to endure all the horrors we had learned about, but would he die? Mixed feelings of relief and fright bounced around my mind. Sister Bobbi, Pastor Art's wife, pulled me aside one night and told me when the right option came, we would know. We would have peace.

and the peace of God, which surpasses all understanding, will guard your hearts and minds through Christ Jesus. (Philippians 4:7)

I could not fathom what Bobbi meant then, but once you experience this peace, you will recognize it. Kind of like having a baby; you recognize labor pains when you feel them. God's peace stretches far beyond our understanding. The absence of tranquility may indicate something is not right for us. The transplant was not in God's plan. We did not understand, but comprehension was not necessary, just trust. We continued to pray for healing.

One day, my friend Cindy called me about a news story. Doctors at Duke Medical Center were using umbilical cord blood rather than bone marrow in transplants. They were obtaining better responses with cord blood since it created less complications than bone marrow. Was this encouraging news our answer to prayer?

Getting a consultation at Duke involved numerous hurdles between Timmy's insurance and his local oncologist. The enemy tried blocking our way, but we refused to quit. Once in Durham, North Carolina, we saw hope for the first time in months. Unlike the first facility, Duke was up-to-date with the most modern equipment and procedures. Many of the terrifying details involved with transplants were nonexistent there, such as the plastic tent and radiation.

Before considering the transplant, the specialist wanted to see how Timmy would respond to interferon. Timmy gave himself a shot of interferon every night for several months. It created flu-like symptoms. Many nights he awoke with chills. I wrapped him in blankets as I held him, speaking words of comfort and praying. Lots of praying. He shivered for hours, but usually he went to work the next day. Timmy could have quit his job and filed for disability, but he wanted to continue working.

We returned to Duke on Valentine's Day 2000. What better way to spend a romantic holiday than to celebrate the great news we would receive? But what awaited us would test our faith. The medicine had not worked because the local oncologist failed to increase the dosage as he should have done. Now, Timmy's white blood count was out of control. Duke's transplant specialist feared Timmy's CML had progressed into blast crisis, the point of no return with leukemia (in 2000, that is). His prognosis: twelve to eighteen months to live, without a transplant.

A half-match cord blood sample was Timmy's only hope. No bone marrow match had been found. The doctor gave Timmy a 65 percent chance of surviving a transplant.

We left Durham with one more thing, the name of a new local oncologist, Dr. Mark Currie.

We ate Valentine's Day dinner at a local restaurant named Honey's. Silence accompanied us during the meal and our three-hour drive home. Once again, dismay overpowered me, but I hid my feelings from Timmy. All sorts of scenarios played out in my mind. "Please help, Lord!"

Timmy took a few vacation days, and we kept our news to ourselves. We filled those days with prayer and precious time together. When my heart felt like it would burst, I slipped outside to prevent Timmy from seeing my trepidation. No need to stress my husband any more than the unbelievable weight already upon him.

Like before, Timmy felt conflicted, and serenity evaded me altogether. Without the transplant, my husband would die. With it, he could still die. Without a miracle, life seemed hopeless.

Three days later, a friend called with our miracle. Heather had watched a news story about an experimental drug labeled STI-571. Yes, another news story we missed. CML patients had gone into remission with this drug, later named Gleevec.

We still had refused to share our desperate news. Those were Timmy's wishes. I would have shouted it from the mountaintops in order for more prayer to ascend to the throne room of God. God didn't need this dear saint to know what had just transpired in North Carolina. Imagine her amazement when we finally clued her in.

Seeing God work in His providence is worth all the sorrow, all the fear, and even the cancer itself. We had hope again. God released us from our pit of despair. He redirected us from south to north. From transplant to an experimental drug trial.

Timmy found a phone number online so I could inquire about the clinical trial. We had to select a major university hospital conducting the study. My heart pounded frantically as they named one hospital after another. Huge distances stood between us and the medical centers until they named Baltimore, Maryland's Johns Hopkins, the only site within driving distance.

Do you remember the night they anointed Timmy? Miracles began happening one after another. Not immediately, but two years later.

The experimental drug performed differently than the usual chemo, which makes people extremely ill. It attacked the cancer cells while leaving healthy cells alone. We went from facing a transplant to a noninvasive drug, with a few irritating side effects. What are a few leg cramps when you are alive? This medication has opened the door for similar medicines to treat various types of cancer.

They accepted Timmy for the clinical trial. Thirty slots had been available for CML patients. Timmy was number thirty.

A bone marrow biopsy revealed Timmy had not advanced into blast crisis. Once the doctor adjusted Timmy's medication, his blood counts stabilized.

The trial required Timmy to keep the other medicine out of his system for two weeks. This was the symptom-controller drug, but without it, his white counts could have dangerously accelerated. God sustained Timmy's white blood count, and it barely rose while he was drug-free.

Another miracle revolved around our safety. We may never realize how much God protected us. Our first trip necessitated a three-night stay, as the protocol for a clinical trial is rigid. Blaring sirens and occasional gunshots made us keenly aware that God guarded us in this high-crime area. It's the only time we have ordered inside a Burger King where bulletproof glass separated us from the cashier.

Timmy began the experimental drug, and within weeks, his blood counts became normal, known as a hematological response. Within two years, the leukemia was undetectable. Nineteen years later, Timmy remains healthy. The drug was FDA approved shortly after the trial. Some people have safely stopped the drug with no problems. This may happen in the future for Timmy. Once again, we will trust God.

Every Valentine's Day brings to mind Valentine's 2000. The day Timmy received his death sentence. The day God told Satan, "Not this time!" God healed Timmy, and we will praise Him forever. Doubt filled our minds many times during those years, but God remained faithful. Through it all, we learned to trust.

"Through it All" is an Andre Crouch song that fits this chapter of our lives.

"I've had many tears and sorrows,
I've had questions for tomorrow,
there's been times I didn't know right from wrong.
But in every situation,
God gave me blessed consolation,
that my trials come to only make me strong.

Chorus:

Through it all,
through it all,
I've learned to trust in Jesus,
I've learned to trust in God
Through it all,
through it all, I've learned to depend upon His Word.

I thank God for the mountains,
and I thank Him for the valleys,
I thank Him for the storms He brought me through.
For if I'd never had a problem,
I wouldn't know God could solve them,
I'd never know what faith in His word could do."*

While doctors and researchers were learning about this miracle drug and its effects on the patients, I was learning about the miracle worker, God. Just like the words in the above song, it was through the trials I learned to trust.

According to Cancer.net, drugs like Gleevec have caused the five-year survival rate for CML to nearly double.

Cancer researchers found a gold mine with these new drugs God used as the means to save Timmy's life. I discovered the most valuable treasure. I learned to trust God. Don't get me wrong, I still haven't graduated yet, but after God healed Timmy, I could always look back on this season.

Look what God did for us! I could rehearse God's trail of miracles. The way the experimental drug came along. The incredible fact that Timmy was accepted as part of the trial at the last minute, filling the last slot. The way God controlled Timmy's blood counts while he was medication-free. And of course, the healing that finally came.

Friend, are you struggling today? Perhaps you feel the way we did. Hopeless. Out of answers. At the end of your rope. At the bottom of a pit.

Maybe your cancer isn't leukemia. Maybe you're not battling cancer, but another disease threatens to rob you or a loved one of many more years. Perhaps your struggle is at the bank, on the job, or inside the courtroom.

That's why you are reading this book. You want deeper faith. You are finished with your emotions calling the shots. Faith is a process, but as long as you make progress in the process, you are headed the right way.

We learn to trust God in baby steps, and that is exactly how Jesus taught the disciples to believe. They had seen miracles, but unbelief remained, hindering their faith. The faith we all need. Faith that believes for a miracle.

Mark chapter eight opens with the feeding of the four thousand. Bear in mind that the disciples had already witnessed the miraculous feeding of the five thousand on a separate occasion. Jesus presented the problem: how do we feed this crowd when we have little food? The people were miles from their homes, and they would have fainted if they attempted the trip without nourishment to sustain them. He tested His disciples. They failed miserably.

Then His disciples answered Him, "How can one satisfy these people with bread here in the wilderness?" (Mark 8:4)

They were in a physical wilderness, in dire need of food. You may be in a different type of wilderness. A medical wilderness. A financial wilderness. A barren wilderness, and it looks as if all hope is gone.

God is our oasis in the wilderness.

You may feel as defeated as those disciples, but hold on, friend:

Faith flourishes in the wilderness.

Jesus was teaching His men to trust Him. To believe in Him. Our wilderness experiences have a purpose.

While Timmy and I were in our wilderness, we learned to trust God. We learned God makes a way when no way exists. He rerouted us from transplant to clinical trial, but the journey got rough. Doubt and fear had a continual presence.

The wilderness will try us, tempt us, but never triumph over us.

Friend, I know the wilderness journey is weary. It frightens us. Without the wilderness, we would miss God's miracles.

Jesus continued by asking the disciples how many loaves of bread they had. Seven loaves, the number of perfection. When we are in our wilderness, we must take inventory of what we already have. The answer might be right before our eyes.

Eyes of doubt see the problem. Eyes of faith see a miracle.

No, we don't have a cure for cancer sitting around the house. We also don't have a million dollars tucked away for a rainy day. We have God, and that is everything.

God can heal the cancer if He wills. God owns the cattle on a thousand hills (Psalm 50:10). He bountifully provides for us. When we have nothing but God, we bless God. We praise God. We trust God.

When we have God, our Father, we also have faith. The problem is that doubt remains. The goal of any wilderness trip is to increase our faith as we decrease doubt. How do we begin?

Face your faith and your Father.

Stop staring at your doubt. The disciples couldn't put their doubt aside for one minute. Didn't they remember? The events were identical. The numbers varied, but the disciples refused to gaze into the eyes of Christ. The eyes of faith.

Jesus repeated the miracle with the loaves as He did with the five thousand. How could these disciples forget? No matter how close we are to Jesus, doubt can blind us. Jesus blessed the bread, giving thanks to God the Father. After the disciples distributed the bread to the four thousand, someone suddenly came up with some fish.

They also had a few small fish; and having blessed them, He said to set them also before them. (Mark 8:7)

Why weren't the fish included with the seven loaves of bread? Did the doubtful disciples hold back the fish just in case the bread did not fill everyone? Do we ever hold out on God? Do we not give Him our all until we see how the Lord will come through? Can we expect God to bless us when we refrain from giving God everything?

After the four thousand ate and returned home, Jesus and His men went to Dalmanutha. There, the Pharisees demanded a supernatural sign from Jesus. Their doubt was different than that of the disciples. They were completely blinded to the truth. The miracles Jesus had already done were not enough for them. Healing blinded eyes, opening deaf ears, and feeding the multitudes weren't sufficient evidence for the hard-hearted Pharisees.

We need to realize that even religious leaders in lofty positions can be unbelievers. Beware of their unbelief. They are not crying out, "Lord, I believe, but help my unbelief." Their cry says, "We refuse to believe."

Jesus and His disciples departed in a boat, but the disciples forgot to pack lunch. Here we go again! Excuse me, Peter, John, and Andrew, how many times do y'all need a retake on this test?

Friend, this is why we can't beat ourselves up for times of faithlessness, fear, and worry. Even the twelve chosen men of Jesus Christ, in His presence, struggled. Of course we will struggle, but we don't give up. We contend for the faith we desperately need.

Doubt may meet you in the wilderness, but faith will lead you out.

Now the disciples had forgotten to take bread, and they did not have more than one loaf with them in the boat. Then He charged them, saying, "Take heed, beware of the leaven of the Pharisees and the leaven of Herod." (Mark 8:14-15)

Jesus warned them about the sin of unbelief. The sin of doubt. We believe in Christ. We believe He will take us to heaven, but we fail to believe He will provide for us today. We believe He forgives sin, but we can't believe He will heal. Believe. Don't believe. That makes us unbelieving believers.

As baby Christians, we muddle through doubt until our faith takes root and grows. Faith is a process. When we see God work, we trust Him more.

Are you making progress in the process?

I reflect on Timmy's battle with leukemia, and I see a woman scared and unbelieving. Twenty years later, God has strengthened my faith immensely. I want you to see that same progression in your life, my friend.

But Jesus, being aware of it, *said to them, "Why do you reason because you have no bread? Do you not yet perceive nor understand? Is your heart still hardened? Having eyes, do you not see? And having ears, do you not hear? And do you not remember?*" (Mark 8:17-18)

Those pitiful disciples still didn't have their spiritual eyes. They still couldn't trust Jesus to meet their needs, even after He had supplied an abundance in food twice.

But we act just like them at times. Let's look at the questions Jesus asked them, and take our own spiritual inventory.

Do we reason too much? Do we trust logic and intellect more than the hand of God? God's ways aren't sensible to man. That is why things don't go the way we expect. God's ways and plans are higher than ours (Isaiah 55:8).

Building an ark when there's never been rain. Nonsense! Parting the Red Sea and walking across on dry ground. Nonsense! Gideon won a battle with trumpets, torches, and clay pitchers. Nonsense. A virgin gave birth to a baby. Fully God, but also fully man. He died to save us from our sins. Nonsense? To man, yes, but not to God.

Do we not perceive or understand? Are we becoming more sensitive to the way God moves, or do we scratch our heads in unbelief? We must look through the eyes of faith, not eyes of doubt. How has God used the illogical in your life?

Are our hearts still hardened like the Pharisees? Before God saved us, we were hard-hearted unbelievers. Examine your growth since then. Unbelieving believers haven't grasped the miraculous ways God moves. Has your heart softened? Are you sensitive to the Holy Spirit?

Then Jesus asked them why they could not perceive the miracles they had witnessed with their five physical senses, especially vision and hearing. They had seen the people fed and collected the leftovers. They had handled the bread, inhaled its aroma, and tasted it. They had been filled because of a miracle. How could they not understand? Had they not heard the Lord's teachings?

Now, we have permission to give the disciples a hard time. Their physical senses had witnessed the miracles, but their spiritual sense wasn't developing. Rarely do we physically witness miracles with our eyes today. We hear testimonies about miracles, but rarely see them in person. I have seen one woman on a cane when she entered a church, and halfway through her message, God healed her. She carried the cane out rather than the cane carrying her. Like the disciples, we must see miracles through our spiritual eyes. Blessed are those who believe not having seen (John 20:29).

Most importantly, do we remember what God has done for us? Do we recall what He has done for others? Survey your life. Look back to the trials God rescued you from. Remember how God has taught you to trust Him. God has been proven faithful. Remember the times He came on the scene right on time. Remember the times He made a way when no way seemed possible. Our answers to these questions will make us keenly aware of what areas we are lacking in and where our faith still needs to take us.

Not all miracles are instantaneous, like my husband's healing. Never give up hope!

Eyes of doubt see the problem. Eyes of faith see a miracle.

We serve the God of all possibilities. He heals as He sees fit: immediately, progressively, through medicine, or surgeries. I love this next passage in Mark because it has similarities to Timmy's healing. Jesus Christ healed many people immediately, but one miracle differed from the rest. The blind man from Bethsaida was brought to Jesus. Like Timmy and me, he wanted healing. Like you, he wanted to be released from his darkness immediately.

44

But Jesus led him out of the town. Jesus wanted to spend time with this man, not because He wanted to learn anything about him, but so the man could learn to walk with Jesus. Could it be that the delay to our breakthrough is simply so we can learn to walk with Jesus? A closer relationship develops as we spend time with the Lord.

He did not see clearly the first time Jesus touched his eyes (Mark 8:22-26).

Jesus asked him what he could see. His response was:

"I see men like trees, walking." (Mark 8:24b)

After Jesus placed His hands on the man a second time, the blind man viewed the world with perfect vision. This is the only recorded progressive miracle in Scripture. Did Jesus have a lesson for us here? Could the man's blindness represent the spiritual blindness discussed in the first part of Mark chapter eight? Could this story be included in the Bible to give us hope when healing does not come immediately? Our faith grows in gradual steps, similar to the way this blind man received his sight. It was a gradual process.

This miracle resembles the majority of miracles we witness today. Healing comes in God's perfect timing.

Trusting God means trusting God's timing.

We want out of our trials, and we want out now, but maybe, as in the above passages, Jesus wants to walk with us for a while. Teaching us to trust Him. Helping us to believe only in Him.

We will never know why Jesus chose to heal this man using a two-step process, but we have learned some life-changing lessons from Mark chapter eight.

Faith is a process. If we don't see progress in the process, something is wrong. If that is the case, don't fret. Ask yourself, have I genuinely been born again? (Chapter One will help you with that.)

Next, examine the root of your doubt. Why don't you trust Jesus to work miracles in your life? Those answers can range from an unanswered prayer to pre-existing doubt. Has someone convinced you miracles have ceased? Prayerfully consider your circumstances and ask God to help your faith increase. Faith is a gift from God. We can't produce it, but we can restrain doubt.

We choose to see through eyes of faith. We choose to close our eyes to doubt.

If you are a new Christian, don't be hard on yourself. Faith is a gradual process. Everybody grows spiritually at different rates, just like our physical bodies grow differently.

If you see progress in the process, celebrate. Praise the Lord for what He is doing in your life. Keep moving in the direction of belief.

Possibly you are in a trial right now. Doubt and fear surround you. Good will arise from this wilderness experience. God will give you beauty for ashes (Isaiah 61:3). You will emerge with more faith. More capable of trusting God to work for the best in your life.

Are you a veteran Christian? Look back at how far God has brought you. Worship Him for the believer He has created in you.

Our faith is growing. Some of us have huge growth spurts while others take baby steps. We understand the purposes of our trials. Faith increases with each storm.

Now that we understand how we will continue to trust God more, we can begin to discover how to fight our fears with faith.

Friend, I am excited about this journey we are on, and I am glad to take it with you. As I close this chapter, I have prayed for you. God is going to do amazing things in our lives. Keep believing!

Heavenly Father, we don't like trials, but we know faith grows in the wilderness. Bestow mercy and grace upon us as we learn to trust You more. In the name of Jesus, Amen.

Stepping Stones

God is our oasis in the wilderness.

Faith flourishes in the wilderness.

Eyes of doubt see the problem. Eyes of faith see a miracle.

Face your faith and your Father.

Doubt may meet you in the wilderness, but faith will lead you out.

Are you making progress in the process?

Trusting God means trusting God's timing.

We choose to see through eyes of faith. We choose to close our eyes to doubt.

Scripture

*Is anyone among you sick? Let him call for the elders of the church, and let them pray over him, anointing him with oil in the name of the Lord. And the prayer of faith will save the sick, and the Lord will raise him up. (*James 5:14-15)

and the peace of God, which surpasses all understanding, will guard your hearts and minds through Christ Jesus. (Philippians 4:7)

But Jesus, being aware of it, *said to them, "Why do you reason because you have no bread? Do you not yet perceive nor understand? Is your heart still hardened? Having eyes, do you not see? And having ears, do you not hear? And do you not remember?* (Mark 8:17-18)

*Songwriters: DARRELL R. BROWN, DENNIS MATKOSKY, DARRELL BROWN

© Sony/ATV Music Publishing LLC, Kobalt Music Publishing Ltd., Warner/Chappell Music, Inc., Universal Music Publishing Group. Data from: LyricFind

THROUGH IT ALL Lyrics - ANDRAE CROUCH | eLyrics.net)

PART II

BREAKING STRONGHOLDS

CHAPTER 4

CHECKING OUR THOUGHTS

Everyone probably has a curiosity as to what I can see. Some are brave enough to ask. My favorite inquiry came from an older man in Gatlinburg.

"Are you legally blind or blind blind?"

I chuckled as I explained how I only see enough to get myself in trouble. This man understood most blind people still have residual sight, even if it is only the difference between light and darkness.

I have learned my vision is deceptive. I recall many times when I was walking with a sighted guide, holding on to Timmy's elbow, and I would come to an abrupt halt. Those painted lines in the Walmart parking lot appeared as if they were standing right in front of my face. I put on the brakes like anyone else would before walking into a wall.

I remember a beach trip to Nags Head, North Carolina when I took several falls in one day. We had been strolling the shoreline in search of seashells, which I did see then. We trudged through the deep sand and finally reached the steps leading us to our hotel. Timmy stopped at the outside shower to wash off his feet. He continued forward as I rinsed the sand from my legs and feet. I started down the sidewalk that led to the hotel. One step stood between me and the hotel sidewalk. Guess who missed the step and landed flat on the concrete? Yes, I did, but I have never forgotten that step since. Figure that one out. I could find seashells, but I couldn't see the step. That's my vision.

That evening, we drove over to Manteo, so Timmy could fish from the Croatan Sound. He left me sitting at a picnic table, but I quickly became bored. This was prior to owning an iPhone with

VoiceOver to entertain me. Before my white cane and many years before Iva.

Unaware that the landscape stair-stepped down to the sound, I stood to my feet and began walking toward Timmy. The first drop-off was about two feet, and I walked right off the edge. The water was low, so I didn't hit the Sound. Just dirt and sand.

I still am misled by my unreliable vision. Just this year, I stooped down to pick something up off the floor. I misjudged my distance from the short bookcase, and I smashed my face right into the top shelf. I walked around with two black eyes for two weeks. Now, I try to bend at the knees and refrain from lowering my head.

Unless you are in a similar situation, your eyes haven't deceived you, but perhaps something else has taken you for a ride. Our world has no shortage of people scamming others out of money. We've all been told lies in order for someone to achieve some gain. We have fallen for offers that were too good to be true. Our minds have tricked us into believing something to be different than it really is.

That happened to me a few years ago. When I am home alone, I do not answer my door. I tell everyone to call before they come. It is a safety precaution since I cannot see who is knocking on my door.

One morning, someone relentlessly pounded on my front door. I stood at the door, and I screamed, "Who is it?"

"I am with Columbia Gas, ma'am."

Likely story. I stepped away from the door to call the police without alerting him. He continued to knock, shouting that he was here to paint our gas meter. In the middle of January? Really? Oh, Mr. Criminal, you are going to find yourself locked up in jail shortly. I had also called Timmy to let him know the cops were on their way to arrest this con artist at our door.

The police arrived and announced themselves so I would open the door. They had checked his identification and credentials. His story, bizarre as it sounded, checked out. A policeman assured me I had done the right thing by calling them, and I should not hesitate to call them in the future.

Then Timmy arrived, and the kind police officers explained the situation to him. He apologized to the Columbia Gas employee and explained that he wanted me to be suspicious. The man began painting, and he had no hard feelings toward me. He seemed quite understanding.

After everything settled down, I offered the gentleman a cup of hot tea or hot chocolate. If he had the ridiculous job of painting gas meters in the middle of winter, offering him something warm to drink was the least I could do. He thanked me and said he was fine. I began washing dishes. The only thing separating us was the kitchen window above the gas meter. I heard him whistling. It sounded familiar. "What a Friend We Have in Jesus." I returned outside and we shared in Christian fellowship.

Due to my circumstances, I did the right thing. Even the man from the gas company agreed. But I perceived something harmless as harmful. How many times does our perception mislead us?

Deception is a warped perception on steroids.

We believe something to be true because someone has beguiled us. They have not only watched our every move, but they have studied it. They have become well acquainted with our weaknesses and know which buttons to push in order to get the desired reaction. They have observed Timmy and me for our twenty-year-plus marriage. They know how to disrupt our calm and create an argument. They know which situations frustrate me, which situations make me sad, and which situations make me fearful. Then they plot to create the perfect storm, causing me to fall prey to their cunningly devised scheme.

Isn't that called stalking? Yes, if it was a human doing the crime, but the culprit I am describing is our enemy, Satan, and his demonic forces.

Most people are mistaken when it comes to old Slew Foot. Some think like I did for many years. He has dictators, terrorists, and serial killers to concentrate on. Surely, Satan has no time for me.

If you are the child of God, he knows you. If you spend time praising the Lord, he knows you. If you fellowship in prayer with God, he knows you. If you live holy, blameless, and righteously, he definitely knows you. If you tell people about Jesus, he knows you quite well.

While Satan cannot break the bond between a believer and God, he will do anything to trip us up and make our lives miserable. He specializes in playing mind games with us, and he is not alone. The world and the flesh also take part in obstructing our focus on God.

Who controls your mind? Before you answer hastily, I want to share a true story with you. I was reminded about this while I listened to a podcast by Brooklyn Tabernacle's Jim Cymbala this morning. I remember the massacre at Jonestown in 1978. I never knew the highly publicized cult leader claimed to be God as Cymbala stated in his message. I googled him and found the red flags that should have warned his followers.

According to Rollingstone.com, Jim Jones moved his church from Indianapolis, Indiana to California to avoid a nuclear attack, which he predicted would occur on July 15, 1967. When the attack never transpired, why didn't members leave his organization? When authorities became suspicious about Jones' activities, he moved his members to Guyana where he continued his brainwashing. His followers were intelligent and multicul-tural, but if they had been familiar with their Bibles, they would have recognized the lies Jones proclaimed.

In November 1978, United States Congressman Leo Ryan and four other people were gunned down by Jones' men at the Port Kaituma Airstrip, after they had visited the compound. Jones proceeded to coax over nine hundred members of the Peoples Temple to drink poisonous Kool-Aid, beginning with the children.

How do knowledgeable people fall for such trickery? The question we should ask ourselves is: what falsehoods are planted in our minds by the world, the flesh, and especially the devil?

The strategic point of satanic attack is the mind. His favorite weapon is deception. In the Garden of Eden, the serpent lured Eve into taking a bite from the forbidden fruit with a lie. If Eve lived in a perfect world where sin had never existed, and she still fell under the sway of the devil, how much more susceptible are we?

Vulnerability to the enemy seems inevitable, but victory is available to the child of God.

When Jesus Christ went to Calvary's cross, He didn't die only as a payment for our sin debt. He defeated the devil. Since the fall of man, Satan had free reign, but Jesus now has all authority (Matthew 28:18). The enemy has been defeated by the blood of the Lamb (Revelation 12:11). God has "...made *us* sit together in the heavenly *places* in Christ," (Ephesians 2:6b). Believers now have the authority over the enemy. Not our own authority, but the authority of Jesus Christ, because we are covered by His blood.

That's right. His blood wasn't shed on that rugged cross just to give us eternal life. His precious blood gave us abundant life.

Satan prowls about like a roaring lion seeking whom he may devour (1 Peter 5:8). We see the lion. We hear his fierce roar, but we are unaware that he is on a short leash. Sometimes the sight of him sends us running. We shrink back in fear and dread. We have forgotten God controls that short leash, and it is perfectly safe for us to move forward rather than cowering away.

That lack of knowledge is the reason many Christians cannot live in victory. The lion puts on a good show, but He was conquered by the Lion of the tribe of Judah.

Sweet friend, begin today by putting the evil one on notice. We live in victory when we live under the authority of Jesus Christ.

The shield of faith and prayer are our spiritual weapons. Pick them up and begin using them, and don't forget the helmet of salvation guards our minds.

We are a society controlled by our emotions. While our feelings aren't evil, they aren't honest either. Worry, doubt, discouragement, despondency, and fear are the ones we will address in this book. Satan attacks our minds to create the emotions that are natural such as fear. But while these are natural feelings, God doesn't want emotions to control us.

Consider anger. That hot temper becomes sinful when left unchecked. It divides families and churches. Animosity harbors unforgiveness and fertilizes the root of bitterness. That irritable passion damages us, not the one we are infuriated with.

What does the Bible say about anger? Hatred and murder stemmed from Cain's wrath toward his brother, Abel (Genesis 4:5-8). The news of Jesus' birth enraged King Herod, and he ordered the slaughter of all male children under the age of two in Bethlehem (Matthew 2:16).

Scripture directs us to be angry and not sin (Ephesians 4:26). The verse continues to warn us about allowing the sun to go down on our wrath. Once we compare our feelings with the truth of God's Word, we understand the necessity to smother our fury.

Overcome anger before anger overcomes you.

We can all agree this is God's way to handle anger. The same is true for any feeling the enemy plants. Let's turn to God's Word:

For though we walk in the flesh, we do not war according to the flesh. For the weapons of our warfare are not carnal but mighty in God for pulling down strongholds, casting down arguments and every high thing that exalts itself against the knowledge of God, bringing every thought into captivity to the obedience of Christ, (2 Corinthians 10:3-5)

Although we are saved, sanctified, and filled with the Holy Spirit, we still live in the flesh. We can't discard it until we reach heaven's gates, but God wants us to realize our warfare is rooted in the spiritual realm.

For we do not wrestle against flesh and blood, but against principalities, against powers, against the rulers of the darkness of this age, against spiritual hosts *of wickedness in the heavenly* places. (Ephesians 6:12)

The fight you had with your spouse this morning. The culprit wasn't your husband or wife, but the enemy. The co-worker you can't get along with. That's the enemy hoping you'll blow a fuse and darken your testimony. That rebellious child. The devil has his hooks in them.

Understanding that the enemy is behind most of our problems can help us defuse them. My husband has a tendency to run late...for everything. When he delays going to church or taking me to a doctor appointment, I want to erupt like Mount St. Helens. Since I have found that the enemy is working behind the scenes in order to get my volcanic reaction, I have learned to bite my tongue. I refuse to give my enemy a front row seat to our marital spat.

Instead, I take the matter to God. I remain silent towards Timmy and smile. Deep inside I am praying, "Lord, do something with this man you have given me."

Then I enter my prayer closet, and I storm heaven with prayers for my husband and his habitual tardiness. I pray about the spiritual forces of darkness who seek to destroy families and sever marriages. That is where the real battle exists, in the heavenly realm.

Paul says the weapons of our warfare are not carnal but mighty in God. We can't win spiritual battles with fleshly or carnal weapons. That's why we never win the argument with our spouses. Rather than employing the fleshly weapon of quarreling, we should engage in the spiritual weapon of prayer. We need God's armor, His weapons that are mighty in pulling down strongholds.

What is a stronghold? In *Victory in Spiritual Warfare*, Dr. Tony Evans defines a stronghold as a pattern with a spiritual root, but the fruit is physical. Dr. Evans states that a stronghold holds you hostage outside God's will. A stronghold can be an addiction such as drugs, sex, food, over-spending, and so forth.

Before every stronghold, there is a foothold.

Satan got his foot in the door when we weren't on guard. He found us isolated, weak, hungry, tired, or sick, and he snuck in. At other times, the enemy attacks after a spiritual victory.

Strongholds become the places where he can do the most damage to our spiritual lives. Satan is able to wage war on the mind by raising "high things." That can be translated as a partition, a dividing wall.

Perhaps your office, school, or church uses a partition to divide a large room into two smaller ones. That is a high thing. My favorite example of this dividing wall is my box of Starbucks Mocha Latte. It has a piece of cardboard dividing the pods and envelopes filled with that chocolate goodness. A partition prevents the pods and chocolate packets from mixing together, keeping my favorite beverage organized. The enemy uses this barrier to make us what James calls a "double-minded" man.

For let not that man think that he shall receive anything of the Lord; he is a double-minded man, unstable in all his ways.
(James 1:7-8)

Unstable definitely describes me when fear or despair take charge. Friend, I imagine you have felt those same unstable pangs. When you are worried about your kids or how to pay the bills. When the illness continues to drag on or life disappoints you in a major way. Maybe your hubby has trouble telling time like mine.

But God doesn't want us unstable. That is why we have this warning in James. God desires steadfast sons and daughters trusting in Him completely.

Satan's partitions are "raised up against the knowledge of God" (2 Corinthians 10:5). The partition deters the godly knowledge from slipping into the other side. Satan tries to block divine information from crossing over to the side where he is attacking.

The side where he may even have control. The side that keeps you afraid. The side that keeps you worried. The side that keeps you discouraged. The side that keeps you in sin. The side that keeps you addicted to whatever is not pleasing to God.

Do you remember that old commercial that told us our minds were a terrible thing to waste? Well, our minds are a terrible thing to give over to Satan. Our thoughts must be God-centered and God-controlled. Not held hostage by the enemy.

The media constantly shapes our minds, whether through television, movies, magazines, social media, or what we discover on the internet. This vast influence is quite persuasive.

Garbage in, garbage out. If something passes through your ear canal or your eye, and it creates an atmosphere conducive to the enemy, that is your warning shot. These are not stray thoughts but deliberate attacks by the enemy of your soul. This is why we must take every single thought captive. Examine it. Compare it to the Word of God.

Finally, brethren, whatever things are true, whatever things are noble, whatever things are just, whatever things are pure, whatever things are lovely, whatever things are of good report, if there is any virtue and if there is anything praiseworthy—meditate on these things. (Philippians 4:8)

Is it true? Is it pure? Is it praiseworthy? Is it obedient to Christ? If not, cleanse your mind from that thought.

Set your mind on things above, not on things on the earth. (Colossians 3:2)

Our minds, and therefore our emotions, can be led astray by thoughts that clutter and distract us from God. We also want to avoid negativity, because it is a welcome mat to the enemy. What are you saying to yourself? I am not good enough. I am not pretty enough. I am not smart enough. What negative thoughts were planted in the fertile soil of your mind from the past? Did someone say you would never amount to anything? Tell God about these unwanted thoughts, and depend on Him to remove them. Tear down the dividing wall.

Paul commanded believers to renew their minds in Romans 12:2:

And do not be conformed to this world, but be transformed by the renewing of your mind, that you may prove what is that good and acceptable and perfect will of God.

Until God gloriously saved us, we were conformed to the world. I was saved in my thirties, and I had adapted to the world's ways. As I matured as a Christian, I became less conformed to the world and began experiencing God's transforming work. However, I never sensed the full extent of the Holy Spirit's transformational power until I began disciplining my thoughts, forbidding those that didn't line up with the truth of God to nest in my head. Actually, it is a daily crucifixion of the thoughts that bombard us.

The world says feeling apprehensive is normal when you lose a job. That's a natural reaction, but Christians have a supernatural Father who has promised to supply our needs (Philippians 4:19). Until we switch from the world's opinion to God's truth, anxiety will plague us until a job is found.

The transformed believer speaks the Word to the problem. The transformed child of God reminds the devil just who Daddy is and tells Satan to go jump in the lake of fire because Daddy will provide. A better job is on the horizon.

The word translated "transformation" is the Greek word "metamorphoo." Paul used this word only one other time in his epistles, in 2 Corinthians 3:18:

But we all, with unveiled face, beholding as in a mirror the glory of the Lord, are being transformed into the same image from glory to glory, just as by the Spirit of the Lord.

Here, Paul teaches us that transformation occurs when we have a face-to-face with the Lord. When we carve out time for God, our minds get aligned with Him.

Radical change occurs when you are radically seeking the presence of God.

Typically, we use the word "metamorphose" when discussing a caterpillar becoming a butterfly. According to scientificamerican.com, the change is a traumatic process. In short, the caterpillar digests itself. Sounds pretty gruesome, but consider the horrific things that have strengthened you. The battles you have won. The obstacles you have overcome. The strongholds that have fallen. The tears you have cried. All have been part of your transformation. You are no longer the person who went into the cocoon of trials. A metamorphosis has happened.

We must resolve today to restrain our emotions tomorrow.

Fear, worry, and doubt no longer have authority. It belongs to us, through Jesus Christ. Trust God in the midst of everything. All of us have experienced circumstances that stirred up anxiety, but now, we will face those overwhelming thoughts in a different light. It will require time and discipline, but when we seek the Holy Spirit's guidance and power, our way of thinking and reacting will change. Begin praying for His leading.

Put yourself under God's microscope to discover your weaknesses. Has God shown you something as you read this chapter? Google Bible verses on that topic and uncover everything the Bible says about it. Select a couple verses to memorize and speak over your life. Speaking the Word of God over yourself is powerful. God only had to speak to bring the world into existence. Use these scriptures on your home screen, or write them on sticky notes, and place them where you will be reminded often.

When that unhealthy idea or emotion grabs your attention, pray. Speak to it. Use your verses, the Sword of the Spirit.

For the word of God is living and powerful, and sharper than any two-edged sword, piercing even to the division of soul and spirit, and of joints and marrow, and is a discerner of the thoughts and intents of the heart. (Hebrews 4:12)

Dear friend, I know you can do this. The devil wants you to think it is too hard, but he wants to keep you bound by his strong-holds. Nothing is impossible with God (Luke 1:37)

Once you begin conquering one thought at a time, one emotion at a time, you will embark upon the freedom of living by faith. You are learning to do battle for the control of your mind. Before long, you'll be walking in victory rather than defeat. When fear arises, you can speak to it and send it running. When you catch yourself slipping back into worry, speak to it. Tell worry it has been evicted.

Life is weighed down with adversities, but we can triumph over our adversary, and allow God to pilot our ships. We cannot grow weary. This battle rages on, but we know the ending. We win! Let that confidence strengthen you as you move forward.

Lord, renew our minds as You see fit. Give us the discipline we need to check our thoughts. Give us wisdom and discernment. Thank You for helping us walk in victory over our enemy. In the name of Jesus, Amen.

Stepping Stones

Deception is a warped perception on steroids.

Vulnerability to the enemy seems inevitable, but victory is available to the child of God.

Overcome anger before anger overcomes you.

Before every stronghold, there is a foothold.

Radical change occurs when you are radically seeking the presence of God.

We must resolve today to restrain our emotions tomorrow.

Scripture

For the word of God is living and powerful, and sharper than any two-edged sword, piercing even to the division of soul and spirit, and of joints and marrow, and is a discerner of the thoughts and intents of the heart. (Hebrews 4:12)

For we do not wrestle against flesh and blood, but against principalities, against powers, against the rulers of the darkness of this age, against spiritual hosts of wickedness in the heavenly places. (Ephesians 6:12)

For let not that man think that he shall receive any thing of the Lord; he is *a double minded man, unstable in all his ways.* (James 1:7-8)

Finally, brethren, whatever things are true, whatever things are *noble, whatever things* are *just, whatever things* are *pure, whatever things* are *lovely, whatever things* are *of good report, if* there is *any virtue and if* there is *anything praiseworthy— meditate on these things.* (Philippians 4:8)

Set your mind on things above, not on things on the earth. (Colossians 3:2)

And do not be conformed to this world, but be transformed by the renewing of your mind, that you may prove what is *that good and acceptable and perfect will of God.* (Romans 12:2)

CHAPTER 5

FEAR MEETS FAITH

I am no stranger to fear, and fear is probably no stranger to you either. When Timmy had leukemia, terror gripped my heart. I tortured myself with disconcerting thoughts. God might allow him to die. Many people lose their spouses. Good people with good spouses, not just unbelievers and evil people. Why would I be any different? I clung to Romans 8:28:

And we know that all things work together for good to those who love God, to those who are called according to His *purpose.*

Even if Timmy died, it would bring God glory. Right? God would work it out for good. Our sovereign, loving God controls everything that occurs to a Christian.

God controls our uncontrollable.

God would take care of me. That was my pep talk. I tried to believe those difficult truths. I knew they were biblical, but in spite of my knowledge, my heart agonized over becoming a young widow. I feared losing my soul mate. I feared our time together would be cut short. I feared living alone with no one to care for me. No one to love me.

Thoughts of life without a spouse by our side send out an alarm. Bells and whistles go off whenever our security is threatened. Sometimes that comes in the form of divorce or illness. The company that shuts down. The bank account that runs dry. Major life changes occur, and with change comes insecurities that cripple us.

Timmy's illness was the first major trial I faced as a Christian. I focused on the worst-case scenario instead of focusing on Jesus. Instead of stressing over days without Timmy, I should have been thanking God for each one I shared with him. Instead of a running list of what ifs, I should have spent my energy on praying for God to heal him. I prayed, but in retrospect, I should have prayed without ceasing.

Years after Timmy's healing, thoughts of life without him still haunted me. My distress intensified as it became clear I had no one to depend on if something happened to Timmy. My insecurities increased as my vision decreased.

Until Iva came into my life, I depended solely on Timmy for almost everything. I went three places without my husband: church, my neighborhood walks, and the ladies room. Otherwise, I stayed home, and I became happy with that life. I hesitated to step out in faith. I still wanted to walk by sight.

When we walk by sight, fear walks with us.

Another source of uneasiness extends from our health crises. We desire strength and wellness, but disease and disabilities interrupt life as we know it. When my vision began its down-ward spiral, I dreaded a life enveloped in darkness. A life where opening my eyes and closing them would make no difference. Praise God, it has never reached that point.

My deepest anxieties occurred when I attempted new things with less sight. You don't need to be visually impaired to feel apprehension about doing something different. Something outside the box. Many people dislike change. New adventures can be fun, but something inside flinches when we think about attempting them.

After I began writing for a ministry, I was invited to several of its women's conferences and retreats. This was uncharted territory. They lovingly encouraged me to attend. As much as I wanted to go, I made excuses to stay home. Instead of admitting the truth, I said I didn't want to attend alone. My inbox blew up with emails inviting Timmy to join me. Many women asked me to sit with them.

I leaned back in my chair as I contemplated the truth. The real reason was that age-old excuse: I needed assistance as a legally blind woman. I had to write those words as I replied to my new friends.

I required assistance getting lunch. Someone needed to walk me to the little girl's room. In a large crowd and an unfamiliar place, I would need help finding a seat. I am comfortable asking for assistance now, but not several years ago, when I felt like a burden to folks.

The ministry head immediately matched me with her precious daughter-in-law, Emily. She had assisted another visually impaired woman before, so she understood my needs. Everyone was attentive. Not like a hovering mother, but like sincere people who love you.

In 2016, Mr. Fear did his best to keep me from our ministry retreat in Myrtle Beach. The plan was to ride with one of the other writers whom I had never met. I would be sharing a three-bedroom suite with two other women. Again, we had never met. I bubbled with excitement each time I thought about spending the weekend with like-minded ladies. What happened?

Jesus had conquered my phobias, or so I thought, but I allowed doubt to cloud my judgment. We listen to the wrong voices sometimes.

"You are really going to ride in a car with a stranger for seven hours? Are you crazy? Do you think these women will take good care of you? This is the first time you have been away from your husband, and in another state! It won't work! You'll go hungry!"

I recognized the enemy's lies, but I could not escape the dark cloud looming over me. The glee of the trip began to slip away. I had to make a decision to listen to the voice of Jesus, as He spoke peace. We have to make that choice because the flesh and the devil are both enemies.

I had a choice. Friend, you have a choice. Listen to the enemy or listen to Jesus.

I prayed and read Scriptures about fear. I set Satan and my flesh straight about who had the authority. Neither of them. And I continued packing for my trip singing praises to God.

The retreat was another blessing, a time of Spirit-filled worship and love. I never went hungry, never sat unattended, and I was never without an elbow to lead me around.

Perhaps you struggle with taking those big steps. The ones that transport us out of our comfort zone. Starting a new school or job. Stepping on an airplane. Traveling abroad.

A potential danger also triggers our warning systems. A natural disaster, a traffic accident, becoming the victim of a crime, or a deadly animal can put us on high alert.

When Iva and I had our first writing retreat in Gatlinburg, Tennessee, we encountered a bear. Reports of a bear on the premises had spread the night before.

I took Iva to a flat, grassy area to use the bathroom. Woods lined one side and a parking area was on the other side. Iva can be stubborn about her bathroom habits.

I heard a "psss!" from the balcony. I turned my head, but no one spoke. I heard it a second time, but nothing else, so I continued urging Iva to go potty.

A minute later, someone whispered loudly, "Hey lady!"

"Yes?"

"There's a bear!"

I screamed and jumped, the things you aren't supposed to do with any wild animal. The bear growled, which shook me to the core. Iva and I raced to the door with my heart thumping. A man coming across the parking lot asked, "Did you see the bear?"

"No, I'm blind!" I shouted.

Safe behind the hotel's door, I listened to see what happened. I heard the parking lot man tell the balcony whisperers I was blind. They didn't realize that, which explains why they said very little. Possibly, they were motioning to the bear with each "Psss."

Before heading to my room, I called Timmy. No answer, but I heard from God. I set reminders on my phone with Bible verses I am memorizing. This verse popped up:

You are of God, little children, and have overcome them, because He who is in you is greater than he who is in the world. (1 John 4:4)

Hearing the verse spoke volumes. The One living within me was definitely greater. Greater than a bear, and greater than Satan. A reminder of a promise I never want to forget. Whatever we face, God is still greater. No matter how afraid we feel, God is greater than anything that strikes a terror in us. John penned this verse in his discourse about spiritual discernment. We have no greater enemy than the Enemy himself, but God is greater. Allow that to sink in, and remind yourself often.

God's protective hand sheltered us from the bear. An army of angels with outstretched swords stood between the bear and us. How do I know that?

That was the scene Elisha's servant saw when he trembled at the sight of the enemy (2 Kings 6:17). Elisha asked God to open his servant's eyes and reveal the invisible. Elisha's servant beheld horses and chariots of fire on the mountains surrounding them. An angelic army. Many times, we go through life with our spiritual eyes closed. Looking through the eyes of faith reveals the supernatural.

Faith sees the spiritual like our eyes see the physical.

Curiosity about fear led me to do some research. Surprisingly, fear literally freezes us. Parts of our brain respond to frightening situations and cause us to freeze, according to gotquestions.org. The freeze response enables a person or animal to determine if their best action is fight or flight in a dangerous situation.

"When prey has been caught and feels helpless, it freezes in order to fake death, which might give it an opportunity to escape... Studies show that particular connections from the periaqueductal grey (brain region located along the spine) to the pyramis at the base of your skull are integral to the freeze response."*

The problem lies within our response to unrealistic concerns. Ones that aren't quite life or death. Like attending conferences with new friends and stepping into uncomfortable territory.

The bear presented a perilous situation, one worthy of a freeze, fight, or flight reflex. I wondered why I could not stop shaking after the incident with the bear. Not a physical shakiness, but an emotional one. It makes sense now. I experienced a rational fear, and I responded naturally.

Normally, we don't continue to quiver after an irrational trepidation, such as public speaking or a dental appointment. Yet, we allow anxious thoughts to hold us captive. We become slaves to fear, and our captor is the enemy.

We cannot live with dread on our horizon, so what do we do? The source of fear is obviously not God.

For God has not given us a spirit of fear, but of power and of love and of a sound mind. (2 Timothy 1:7)

Paul knew Timothy experienced some alarm. Being a preacher in those days put a target on his back. While in a Roman prison, awaiting execution, Paul commanded Timothy to avoid troubling thoughts.

You would think Paul might have said, "Run Timothy! Don't preach the gospel, except to your friends!"

But Paul loved God, and he would rather die for the sake of the good news than live as a coward.

Fear comes from either Satan or our flesh. Whenever we are afraid, we must learn to quickly recognize the source. Instead of focusing on our nightmare, we must concentrate on what God has given us: power, love, and a sound mind.

We should heed Paul's advice to Timothy. Before Jesus ascended to heaven, He told His disciples (and us) we shall receive power once the Holy Spirit comes upon us (Acts 1:8). A Christian filled with the Holy Spirit has power. We may not feel powerful at times, but our feelings lie. We must stop depending on our emotions and start leaning on God.

Paul told the Ephesians:

Now to Him who is able to do exceedingly abundantly above all that we ask or think, according to the power that works in us, (Ephesians 3:20)

Look at that verse. Where is this power? That's right. It is already in us! Not in heaven waiting, but the power resides in us now. We just need to move the flesh and the devil out of the way. That's what we do when we choose faith over our emotions.

What would you ask God in a fearful situation? Don't allow my husband to die! Heal me from this condition that has wrecked my life! Give me the all-sufficient grace to live with it! Give me the courage to broaden my horizons! Will You journey this new path with me? Protect and watch over us today. If evil approaches, will You hide us under Your wings?

But Paul says God is able to do exceedingly abundantly above all that we ask or think. No matter what our prayer requests include, God is able to do abundantly and exceedingly much more. He can do what we cannot imagine. And that power resides within us, because we are the temples of the Holy Spirit.

Ask big. We have a big God.

Many years ago, my husband was an avid bear hunter. I asked him if he was afraid. Confidently, he replied, "No, because I was carrying something more powerful than the bear."

His reference was to a high-powered rifle. Christian, we have something more potent in us, the Holy Spirit.

Love was the next gift Paul reminded Timothy about. We don't become fainthearted because we are loved by a Father who protects us. Nothing will happen to us outside the will of God. Staying in His will assures us of His safeguard on our lives.

Christians extend love to others. Missionaries operate from a spirit of love rather than fear, despite the dangers that surround them. Even witnessing to friends, family, and strangers can arouse uneasiness, and sometimes we back out, giving way to the enemy. Our love for God and our love for mankind should conquer the dismay preventing us from spreading the gospel.

I never feared writing, publishing books, or even public speaking. When God placed those callings on my life, I eagerly wanted to serve Him. However, some preachers are terrified of standing before a crowd, but the spirit of love erases any qualms they may have.

Finally, Paul tells Timothy that God gives us a sound mind. That can be translated as discipline or self-control, another fruit of the Spirit. This is in contrast to the spirit of fear. Fear creates panic, but a sound mind creates peace. Fear produces instability and insecurity, but a stable mind rests securely in Christ.

In the last chapter, we discussed the high things Satan raises up against us. Fear often becomes an emotional stronghold. It consumes our lives as well as the situations that evoke it. Until that stronghold is broken down, it takes control of our minds and subsequently, our lives.

Are you circumstance-controlled or Christ-controlled?

The Apostle Paul has taught us God isn't the source of fear. When I have choices to make, I can almost guarantee the choice that creates some uncertainty is the right decision because Satan is cleverly hoping I will choose the other one. Paul also taught us we have the power of the Holy Spirit, the love of God, and a sound mind. All of which have no resemblance to apprehension. Now let's look at one of my favorite verses about fear.

Fear not, for I am with you;
Be not dismayed, for I am your God.
I will strengthen you,
Yes, I will help you,
I will uphold you with My righteous right hand. (Isaiah 41:10)

The command to abstain from fear comes with promises. God never abandons us. He promised He would never leave us, and He would never forsake us (Hebrews 13:5). No matter what we endure, we will never be alone. God walks every mile beside us. God is present through the flood and the fire. God keeps His promises, so why should we be dismayed?

Second, God reminds us of His characteristics. He is not a far-off god. He is the Creator of the universe, our all-powerful, all-knowing, all-encompassing Abba (Father). Consider His awesome greatness! In spite of all His great characteristics, He has a uniquely intimate relationship with each of us. Anytime you are prone to tremble, remember our great God is your Daddy.

Isaiah also tells us God strengthens us. He fills our fuel tanks when we feel weak. We can do all things, anything through the strength of Jesus (Philippians 4:13). Apart from God, we are weak, but His strength is accessible when we need it most.

Next, God is our helper. We can go one better than Isaiah. The Helper, the Holy Spirit, lives in modern-day Christians. Before Jesus' resurrection and ascension, the Holy Spirit never took up permanent residence in believers (1 Samuel 16:13-14; Psalm 51:11; John 14:16-17; Ephesians 4:30). When comparing the gospels to the book of Acts, we clearly see the boldness of the apostles. This group of little-faith men constantly blundered while with Jesus. In Acts, they resonated the indwelling force of the Holy Spirit. We have our help 24/7, divine help, not earthly help. Imagine what we can conquer and accomplish through the power of the Holy Spirit. We touched on that earlier in this same chapter.

Finally, God upholds us in His righteous right hand. Though we may fail. Though we may fall. Though we feel the earth sinking beneath us, He holds on to us. We are secure in His mighty hands.

Isaiah has given us five reasons never to shrink back again: God's abiding presence, His attributes, His strength, the Holy Spirit's indwelling power, and God's ability to uphold us. Let's look deeper at faith now.

Now faith is the substance of things hoped for, the evidence of things not seen. (Hebrews 11:1)

"Faith is the substance of things hoped for," but the New International Version (NIV) says, "faith is the confidence in what we hope." We understand the word "confidence" better than "substance." Confidence means we know, without a doubt, things will work out for our good and God's glory. We are confident in God because He is trustworthy. Confidence is void of doubt.

The NIV continues by saying faith is "assurance about what we do not see." Faith is evidence. Faith is proof of what we cannot see. Despite our inability to see it, faith gives us the assurance we need. If we could see it, it wouldn't be faith.

I cannot see many things, but that doesn't mean they are nonexistent. Faith believes in something unseen. Faith believes it will see God at work. Faith gives us a set of spiritual eyes. It is not faith alone, but it is the one we have faith in.

As horrific events and thoughts enter our lives, let's rest in the fruit of the Holy Spirit: power, love, and a sound mind. We have already received everything we need to banish those scary thoughts. So, let's put it in action.

When we fear, we lack faith. Where there is faith, fear flees. Where there is fear, there is no faith. Where there is faith, there is no fear. They cannot coexist.

Fear freezes, but faith frees.

Fear is Satan's tactic to derail us from God's blessings. He uses it to prevent us from serving God like we should. It is an emotion from a deceitful heart. We find ourselves in hard places that arouse panic. Fright is a natural response, but we cannot camp out there. Rather than wallow in despair, we should worship God. We spend way too much time in a place God never designed for us to linger.

We must choose faith. Choose to move on in the face of timidity. Choose to rely on God. Kick every doubt to the curb and believe God will heal that sick spouse or child. Believe God will open the door to a new job. Believe God will free us from our financial prison. Believe God will enable us to tell people about Him. Believe God in the storm. Believe God in the face of danger.

When we choose faith, we will walk in victory. We will rest in peace, not cringing. We will have a testimony to share with the world. God came through. God made a way. God will give us victory through faith (1John 5:4).

As we endure trials, our faith grows. Just like all the Bible folks we read about, we can conquer the spirit of disquietude. They had no super faith pill. We have everything they had. Even more, we have the Holy Bible.

Faith is Noah cutting down trees and sawing them into lumber when he had not seen rain. Faith is Abraham raising the knife above his son, Isaac, when God commanded him to sacrifice his son, but God provided a ram instead. Faith is Moses demanding Pharaoh to let God's people go.

Faith is Rahab hiding the Israelite spies, putting her life in danger, but being rescued when the walls of Jericho tumbled down. Faith is Gideon fighting the Midianites with three hundred men using trumpets, torches, and pitchers as their weapons. Faith is Ruth following Naomi to Bethlehem.

Faith is Hannah praying and believing God would grant her a son, Samuel. Faith is David fighting Goliath with nothing but a slingshot and the Lord. Faith is Esther approaching the king on behalf of the Jews.

Faith is Daniel sleeping in the lion's den. Faith is the three Hebrews refusing to bow down to Nebuchadnezzar, facing the fiery furnace only to come out unscathed. Faith is Jonah in the belly of the fish believing God would set him free.

Faith is the centurion telling Jesus He can heal his servant from afar. Faith is the woman with the issue of blood who believed she only had to touch Jesus' garment to be healed. Faith is Peter climbing out of the boat and walking on water.

Faith is Jesus facing the cross because of His great love for us. Faith is Peter and John refusing to obey man rather than God. Faith is Phillip leaving the crowds when God directed him to the desert for a divine meeting.

Faith is Paul boldly proclaiming the gospel in Jerusalem knowing it might mean his death. Faith is Onesimus, the runaway slave, returning to Philemon.

Faith is answering God's call and writing books no one may purchase. Faith is learning to live in a potential world of darkness.

What happens when we walk in faith? Our hope in God gets a boost. We realize we can trust Him with our lives. Sometimes we must endure some pretty horrific things to get our faith tanks full.

Faith lives in peace while fear lives in panic.

We will always endure seasons that make us afraid. On my last trip to Gatlinburg, the bears were roaming. When we checked in, the desk clerk frightened the life out of me. Enough that I considered returning home with Timmy, rather than staying for my ten-day writing retreat.

I recognized the plot of Satan. As I sat in the car waiting on Timmy to finish shopping, I found Scripture about fear. As I spoke each verse over myself, I felt the chains begin to drop. A peace began to settle me. God walks before me clearing the path.

Before Timmy left Iva and me, we talked to the hotel mainte-nance man. He assured me we were in no danger. Park rangers had tranquilized four bears the week before we arrived. They hauled them far into the mountains. Now, the two bears who remained were so accustomed to people that they only sought food, not trouble. My church had been praying, and we know God providentially worked to move those other bears away just in time for this special season I had planned with Jesus.

When fear knocks on your door, let faith answer. When we choose faith, it thaws us from the frozen state of fear and we will see the Spirit's power at work. We will see how God brings us through the disease, the disability, and the dilemma. Our comfort zone cowardice will vanish. God's power will chase panic away, leaving peace in its place.

Pray and speak Scripture out loud. This clears the clutter of lies that entangle our minds, leaving us unable to move on for God. As you read each verse, you will hear each chain break and hit the floor. God desires our complete confidence. He has proven Himself faithful time and time again.

Now you've learned the enemy's schemes. Instead of allowing fear to dominate you, you can dominate fear. You carry the weapon that is sharper than any two-edged sword, and you know how to wield that sword, the Word of God.

Never be the victim of fear again. Never allow its crippling effects. How much more can we accomplish for the kingdom of God when we slam the door on fear? How much better will we sleep at night when faith rules in our hearts? What powerful testimonies will we have to share?

What if these victories spread through our families? Our churches? Our communities? We are no longer immobilized by this dreaded emotion. We are warriors of faith!

Whatever grips you now, God's got you. He holds you in loving, merciful arms. He will strengthen you. As you draw close to Him.

Lord Jesus, help my friend reading this chapter. I know those feelings of dismay. I also know they don't come from You. We have been afraid so long, we don't know how to conquer it. But it is possible through You. I speak to that fear and demand it to be removed. Help my friend trust in You and have victory. In Jesus' name, Amen.

Stepping Stones

God controls our uncontrollable.

When we walk by sight, fear walks with us.

Faith sees the spiritual like our eyes see the physical.

Ask big. We have a big God.

Are you circumstance-controlled or Christ-controlled?

Fear freezes, but faith frees.

Faith lives in peace while fear lives in panic.

When fear knocks on your door, let faith answer.

Scripture

And we know that all things work together for good to those who love God, to those who are called according to His purpose. (Romans 8:28)

You are of God, little children, and have overcome them, because He who is in you is greater than he who is in the world. (1 John 4:4)

For God has not given us a spirit of fear, but of power and of love and of a sound mind. (2 Timothy 1:7)

Now to Him who is able to do exceedingly abundantly above all that we ask or think, according to the power that works in us, (Ephesians 3:20)

Fear not, for I am with you;
Be not dismayed, for I am your God.
I will strengthen you,
Yes, I will help you,
I will uphold you with My righteous right hand. (Isaiah 41:10)

Now faith is the substance of things hoped for, the evidence of things not seen. (Hebrews 11:1)

- https://www.gotquestions.org/faith-vs-fear.html

CHAPTER 6

FROM WORRY TO WORSHIP

Do you struggle with worry? All mommas just shouted a loud "Amen!" I conducted my own survey on Facebook, and I discovered that children were the main source of anxiety. Next came parents and family.

For the first eighteen years of my daughter's life, she was my primary reason to worry. Finances held the number two spot, and during Timmy's leukemia crisis, those concerns prevailed. I knew worry was sinful. It says, "I don't trust You with this, God."

During the season of Timmy's cancer, I had numerous bills to manage. Either our insurance company denied the claim or it was never submitted. Many times, insurance had previously covered the charges for the same service. I knew they should pay it again, but this fight had to play itself out over and over again.

I began praying over the bill, calling insurance to have the same conversation we had before, and sticking the bill in my filing cabinet. As I shut the drawer, I reminded God I was trusting Him to handle it.

That is my first memory of handling those nagging thoughts correctly. Yet, I still remained anxious where my daughter was concerned, especially when she began driving. She worked at a local pizza place, about seven miles from home. She had to call me when she arrived at work. Then, I demanded she call me before leaving. It was a fifteen-minute trip, and if it took any longer, Momma became overly concerned. I would call her wanting to know she was safe. Then, the unthinkable happened. Something worse than a minor accident.

Two of her co-workers, a married couple in their thirties, drew her into their tangled web of perversion. They dangled the bait, and she was ready to bite. They lured her from a Christian home. They purposely waited until her eighteenth birthday to strike, like a venomous snake.

Under their influence and filled with their poison, she walked out of the house one day. Never to return. I tried convincing her to come home. Sister Bobbi tried, but we both received the same reply, like a recording: "I've made my decision. I am moving out."

Timmy and I took her by the arm and tried to coax her to get in our car. Since we touched her, she obtained protective orders on both of us. No evidence necessary. Just a touch. Now, she would have me arrested if I even called her.

What was I going to do? The momma who needed to know she was safe couldn't contact her at all. I didn't know where she lived, but before long, they all moved to Charlotte, North Carolina.

Worry became the least of my problems. I slipped into a severe depression, and I came close to taking my life. If I were going to hold onto my sanity, I could no longer concern myself about her whereabouts or safety. I had more serious issues at hand, and any additional despair would send me over the edge. I released her into God's hands where she always was all along.

Mommas often consume themselves with worry rather than depending on God. I know it is hard not to be cautious with these cherished gifts from God, but we have to trust our heavenly Father. Truth be told, He loves them more than we do. More than we are capable of loving them. God helped me to keep that stinking thinking at a safe distance.

I wish I could tell you the Scriptures I am about to share carried me through those horrendous months, but it was a song by Jeff and Sheri Easter, called "Praise His Name."

When everything falls apart praise His name
When you have a broken heart raise your hands and say
Lord, You're all I need, You're everything to me
And He'll take the pain away

When it seem you're all alone praise His name
When you feel you can't go on just raise your hands and say
Greater is He that is within me
And you can praise the hurt away if you'll just praise His name.*

Knowing the lyrics of this song lined up with the Word of God, I was transported from worry to worship. Even though depression had settled upon me, I knew I had to praise God. I didn't feel like praising. I didn't want to worship, but God doesn't say we have to feel like it. He just tells us to praise Him.

Out of our ashes arise beautiful praise.

God knows our hearts. He holds the shattered pieces in His hand. As our praises reach Him, He knows the strength it took for us to utter them.

Whenever I got misty-eyed, I praised the Lord, and He wiped the tears away. I sang hymns, and I made up some songs. Each time my thoughts visited my precious daughter, I turned to worship.

Worship chases worry away.

I found praise acted as a pain reliever. Instead of allowing myself to look at my bleak situation, I looked at my big God. Instead of wondering where my daughter was or what she was doing, I trusted God with her life. And my heart.

What keeps you awake at night? Which thoughts torment you when you wake up? What keeps your mind preoccupied? Has your worry accelerated to the point of panic attacks and other related health problems?

Is it your children? Is it a normal concern about their health, their marriage, or their jobs? Maybe it isn't your kids, but your parents. Their health is failing. Things at work aren't going well. Perhaps your own health is worrisome.

Could it be those financial woes? Some are quite serious, but many keep us distressed because we really doubt God will supply our needs (Philippians 4:19).

Are your concerns on steroids? They are out of control. They zap your energy and your peace.

Worry not only affects our minds, but it has physical effects. According to https://chopra.com/, it can be the source of headaches, nausea, muscle tension, exhaustion, irritability, and difficulty concentrating and making decisions.

Five hundred years ago, Michel de Montaigne said: "My life has been filled with terrible misfortune; most of which never happened."

The same article discussed a study where they found that 85 percent of the things people worried about never happened, leaving only 15 percent that did. From that 15 percent, subjects in the study reported that in almost 80 percent of those cases, they handled the circumstances better than they thought they could, or it was a worthwhile lesson. The study concluded that 97 percent of our worries are exaggerated and misperceptions. The writer went on to add that worry causes our brains to produce a stress hormone. These hormones shrink brain mass and lower the IQ. Worriers are also prone to heart disease and cancer.

Along with the emotional and physical consequences, that troublesome clutter in our brain has spiritual effects. Worry is sinful, and sin interferes with our prayers and blessings.

May I take you back to a Roman prison during the first century? While chained to a guard, Paul wrote a letter to the church at Philippi. It has been called "the joy epistle."

Paul begins by exhorting believers to "...stand fast in the Lord, ..." (Philippians 4:1b). This refers to stability. Notice how that word continues to pop up in every passage of Scripture we study, whether the topic is strongholds, fear, or worry? God is telling us stability is an absolute necessity. Anxiety does not give us stability. Far from it. It will bring us down faster than the ocean waves of a hurricane destroying a fishing pier. And like that pier when it crashes into multiple splintered pieces, we crumble under the pressures of our angsts.

We fidget. We can't sit still. Our minds refuse to concentrate. Our tummies do somersaults. Years ago, I was a "Jell-O Christian" as Pastor Art used to call it. I jiggled every time my life hit a speed bump.

Paul tells us how we can conquer those jitters and become level headed. "In the Lord." A self-help program will not do the job. A pep talk won't cut it, and pretending it doesn't exist won't fix it. We can only obtain steadfastness through the Lord.

The only firm foundation believers have is found in Jesus Christ. All others are like the shifting sand.

Paul also instructed his readers to stand against the attacks of the devil. We suit up in God's armor (Ephesians 6:11). This is war, and we must stand our ground. Take those thoughts captive and examine them. Worry, like fear, doesn't come from God. God has our dilemmas worked out long before they unfold before our eyes. Worry tells Him we want to reverse the roles and play the role of Father for a season.

Let Daddy be Daddy.

He can handle our trials much better than we ever could. We must refuse to pick them up. Let's leave it all at the foot of the cross.

Perhaps the source of unrest in the Philippian church centered around two quarreling women. Paul addresses these women, and then he penned the greatest words ever written to calm our nervous souls.

Rejoice in the Lord always. Again, I will say, rejoice!

Let your gentleness be known to all men. The Lord is at hand.

Be anxious for nothing, but in everything by prayer and supplication, with thanksgiving, let your requests be made known to God; and the peace of God, which surpasses all understanding, will guard your hearts and minds through Christ Jesus. (Philippians 4:4-8)

Paul had already commanded us to stand fast, and now he wants us to rejoice. At first glance, we may not see any connection between stability and joy, but joy is a vital ingredient if we are going to live unshakable lives. When we rejoice, we rise far above our crises. Just like the command to stand fast in the Lord, Paul tells us to rejoice in the Lord.

Joy isn't the absence of problems, but the presence of God.

Joy isn't in our worries. Joy isn't in our circumstances. Joy isn't in our sickness. Joy isn't in our grief. Joy isn't in a bounced check. But joy is in Jesus!

Jesus is in control of our lives. He is sovereign over all things. Despair sets in when our minds wander to the what ifs. What if the surgery doesn't help? What if I lose my job? What if the things don't work like we want them to?

Hello, my name is Carolyn and I am a recovering control freak. I can't control life's upsets. As long as things run according to plan, I feel totally in control, but when the fierce winds blow, I realize how little control I really do have.

We can rejoice in Jesus because we can't control that cancer, but Jesus can. We can't control the safety of our children, but Jesus can. We can't control the medical bills or the company shutdown, but Jesus can.

When we embark upon worship as I did in those dark days, our focus changes. We appreciate God for all He is. God is good. God is love. God is merciful and kind. He is creator, sustainer, healer, and He is our strength. We give thanks for His blessings: Our homes. Our health. Our kids. Our freedoms. Our jobs. When we pray to Jehovah Jireh, the Lord who provides and to Jehovah Rohe, our shepherd, we remember how great our God is. And how small our concerns are when compared to Him.

We rejoice in the Lord, so we must trust in the Lord. If we are going to stand firm and find joy in Jesus, we need to intimately know Jesus. That requires spending valuable time in His presence. We don't usually realize that until something goes wrong. Then we are left spiraling out of control. That is where I found myself the day my daughter left home.

Our third command from the imprisoned apostle is to let our gentleness be apparent to all. "Epieikes" is the Greek word translated gentleness in verse five. *Vine's Complete Expository Dictionary of Old and New Testament Words* defines it as patience. In Max Lucado's book *Anxious for Nothing: Finding Calm in a Chaotic World*, he says it means levelheaded or steady. That is in stark contrast to instability, nervousness, and despair. It is calm rather than chaos. It is peace rather than panic.

Are we holding it all together while we are shopping, only to have a meltdown at home? Or is our out-of-control displayed at the workplace, the source of much stress? Perhaps we look the part at church, but after Sunday at noon, our fretfulness returns.

Paul reminds his readers that the Lord is at hand, giving us a reason to exhibit gentleness. The Lord's presence is constantly with us. At the mall, at the job, at church, and at home. When we are reminded of His continual nearness, tranquility should flood our souls. You are with me, Lord. I don't know what will happen, but You are by my side through all of it.

The Lord is at hand also refers to His second coming. The knowledge that one day quite soon Jesus will take us home to live eternally reassures us these worldly troubles are only temporary when compared to eternity.

Paul has directed us to be stable, joyful, and calm Christians. Now comes the climactic section in this passage.

Be anxious for nothing, but in everything by prayer and supplication, with thanksgiving, let your requests be made known to God; (Philippians 4:6)

The same word translated "anxious" here in Philippians was translated "worry" in Matthew 6:25, when Jesus forbade us to worry:

"Therefore I say to you, do not worry about your life, what you will eat or what you will drink; nor about your body, what you will put on. Is not life more than food and the body more than clothing?"

When Jesus delivered His Sermon on the Mount, where we find this passage, clothing and food were sources of great concern for the Israelites. They lived simple lives. I remember when I had no telephone. Not a cell phone, but no phone in the house either. I remember picking up three TV channels on something called an antenna on the roof. You younger folks can google "rabbit ears on a TV" and see how we got reception before cable TV. I also recall living without air conditioning. I wonder if I could return to that simple life. No computer. No microwave. Now, I get frustrated when the internet goes out or my phone dies. Most of us live such comfortable lives that we consider it an immense annoyance when those comforts are removed, even for a short time.

Another source of worry centers around our future. Things that may never happen. We see people wringing their hands in anguish, and we think it is normal. For unbelievers it is normal, but it is abnormal for the children of God. Our heavenly Daddy takes care of us. Why is it so difficult for us to allow Him to do His job?

Although I have successfully turned my daughter over to God, I still find myself picking up something else to toss around in my mind. When my calendar is void of speaking engagements, I start brainstorming. Some planning isn't bad, but I go overboard. I continually search for new ways to make my name available. I pray for invitations to come in. Rarely do I consider the fact that God has me in a quiet time to nurture me. I fail to consider God is giving me time to finish writing this book.

Recently, a large unexpected expense wiped out two-thirds of the money I had reserved for editing this book. It wasn't even the full amount I needed to start with, not to mention the formatting and cover design expenses. A self-published author like myself incurs all the expenses traditionally published authors don't encounter. As I began to focus on the funds I lacked, I stopped myself. I got off my shaky foundation and stepped onto the solid rock. I praised God for how this will work out, and I prayed, "Lord, if You want this book published, You will have to do something. I will continue asking. I will continue seeking, and I will continue knocking. But I refuse to worry. I trust You to provide the funds in the name of Jesus, Amen."

I trust God to provide, and when He does, I am going to turn back to this page, even if it has already been edited, and I am going to describe how God moved.

Prior to editing, I received an unexpected check, plus some book sales. All things working together. God ultimately provides.

Did you see how I handled that? I stopped being anxious, and I prayed with thanksgiving. I did exactly what Philipians 4:6 says. Don't worry. Pray. Don't be anxious. Pray. Don't fret. Pray.

Pray about everything. Nothing is too small or too big to take to God. If you are a parent, you want your children to approach you with their difficulties. God feels the same way. The only difference is He can fix everything if He so desires. As human parents, our ability to fix things has limitations. We are blessed to have a Father who wants us to cast our cares on Him. Many times, we refuse to go to God. We don't have because we don't ask (James 4:2-3). What blessings have we missed out on because we didn't ask big?

We think too small. We don't want to sound greedy. We limit our blessings when we don't pray about everything.

We stand. We rejoice, and we pray. The result will be a peace that is beyond human comprehension.

Pray before you protest.

How many times do we complain and pout when storms arise? I am probably batting 100 percent on that one, but I am trying to change that faulty first response. Our initial reaction to problems should be prayer, not protest.

We must consider the tribulations we face are for our good and God's glory. That doesn't make them any easier, but things run smoother when we cooperate with God and allow Him to do His perfect refining work. He will cover us with a peace the world doesn't grasp, but they will surely take notice. It is the peace of Jesus Christ (John 14:27). It is the fruit of the Holy Spirit (Galatians 5:22). Claim this promise. Speak the words over your life. Put it on the fridge or on your phone. Memorize it, and pray it. When we pray, the answer might be delayed, but the peace is immediate.

Prayer is the passageway to peace.

That peace will guard our hearts and minds until the answer arrives. His peace shields us from sleepless nights. It is a deterrent to stress. Peace clears the clutter of chaos. It calms the pounding heart. It sets us on firm ground.

A few years ago, Timmy woke me during the night. He had just gone to bed when he began struggling to breathe. My first response was to call 911, but he wanted me to wait. I laid my hands on him, and I prayed. Then he told me to make the call. EMTs sat in my living room working on him. I felt like I was outside my body. I can't explain it. I remained calm through it all. I was totally covered in a supernatural peace I had never experienced before.

Once we arrived at the emergency room, they administered a breathing treatment and medication to Timmy. His blood pressure had risen to the extent that it was pushing fluid into his lungs, a flash form of congestive heart failure.

Timmy came home several days later, with more blood pressure medications. The best outcome is that he takes better care of himself now. The tranquility that overwhelmed me that night was the divine peace of God. It is the promise in Philippians chapter four.

You might be wondering if it is possible for you to possess this unbelievable peace. You might feel a life void of worry is unrealistic. Sweet friend, it is absolutely possible, but you must be willing to banish those distressing thoughts from your mind, like we discussed in Chapter four.

Removing our worries necessitates trust in God. A wholehearted faith in the Lord diminishes our misery. Trusting God should be the easiest thing in the world for Christians. Our enemy doesn't want us to enjoy that confidence. He wants to shake up our lives. The world believes worry is a normal part of life. While it is part of an unbeliever's life, it has no place in the lives of believers. Our flesh is programmed to dwell on uncertainties. We are new creations now, and we must overrule our flesh.

We trust God. We stand firm. We worship, especially in the face of trouble. We put up a "Do Not Enter" sign over our hearts. And we pray.

Down on our knees, we battle for our minds.

We will dress in our spiritual armor, and we will experience victory. We possess the promise of peace. God is faithful to fulfill His promises.

Friend, I want to challenge you today. Prayerfully consider what your worries are. Write them down. Then one by one, take them to God. Remember to do it with a grateful heart because you believe God is going to work in your life. You believe your breakthrough is coming. Thank Him like it has already happened.

Praise the Lord. Worry can't hang around in a heart filled with worship. Praise God for your many blessings. Praise Him for being your Father.

As you feel each burden lifting from your shoulders, commit to let it go. Do not leave your prayer closet and pick that burden up. If this becomes a struggle for you, you may want to fast. Many of us have a tough time letting it go. It is a foreign concept, and a time of fasting and prayer will bring you closer to Christ.

We can obtain the abundant life when we evict worry. Will it be easy? No, you must be committed, but look at the end results.

Can you envision a life free of those pests that rob you of peace, sleep, and joy?

All things are possible with Jesus Christ. We secure healthier, richer, and well-balanced lives when we heed the Word of God. So, let's get busy. We have some house cleaning to do in our minds.

Heavenly Father, forgive us for the sin of worry. We would rather leave it all in Your capable hands, but we struggle with that. We aren't happy with worry, and we aren't happy without it. We want Your peace. Help us become stable. We praise You because we believe You will remove our anxious thoughts. In Jesus' name, Amen.

Stepping Stones

Out of our ashes arise beautiful praise.

Worship chases worry away.

Let Daddy be Daddy.

Joy isn't the absence of problems, but the presence of God.

Pray before you protest.

Prayer is the passageway to peace.

The battle for our minds will be fought on our knees.

Scripture

Be anxious for nothing, but in everything by prayer and supplication, with thanksgiving, let your requests be made known to God; (Philippians 4:6)

"Therefore I say to you, do not worry about your life, what you will eat or what you will drink; nor about your body, what you will put on. Is not life more than food and the body more than clothing?" (Matthew 6:25)

- http://www.songlyrics.com/jeff-sheri-easter/praise-his-name-lyrics/

- https://donjosephgoewey.com/eighty-five-percent-of-worries-never-happen-2/

CHAPTER 7

RISING ABOVE DISCOURAGEMENT

I placed my hand on the doorknob, opening it barely enough to confirm the hissing noise was the hotel sprinkler system watering the grass. Iva had finished her breakfast and couldn't wait to go potty any longer. Unfamiliar with sprinkler systems, I decided to maneuver between them. A blast of icy water shot up my leg and onto my back. I definitely was awake now. I darted past the little showerheads taking target practice at me and Iva. We failed to dodge them, but Iva managed to potty. Soaked, we went back to our room to dry off.

I called Timmy. "How long do sprinkler systems run?"

"About twenty minutes or so. Why?" Timmy responded.

He erupted into laughter when I explained what happened.

"I'm glad you think it is funny. It felt like it was raining from hell," I replied.

More laughter.

Sometimes, our lives feel as if it is raining from hell. The car breaks down. An unusually high and unexpected bill greets you in the mailbox. The oven stops working on the night of that special dinner. Your illness the doctors can't seem to understand continues, and now the kids are sick. One problem after another arises, and we feel disheartened.

If you are human, you have felt the weight of discouragement. It affects everybody, showing no favoritism. No one wants to feel down, even depressed, but Christians might be ashamed to admit they are not feeling the joy of the Lord as they should.

Jesus is our sole source of joy, but the world, the flesh, and the devil try to cover us with a dark cloud. Joy and happiness aren't equals. Happiness is based on happenings.

"Joy has its springs deep down inside. And that spring never runs dry, no matter what happens." - S.D. Gordon

Discouragement isn't as dark as depression, but it can be the stairway that leads us there. Especially if we have the genetics or chemical makeup for it. Have you ever felt as if you were drowning in the sea of discouragement? When I was desperately trying to believe God would improve my vision through cataract surgery, pessimism surrounded me. People spewed their doubt, making it a difficult season for me. When the devil wasn't questioning the logic of my faith, the unbelief of others tried attaching itself to me, like a bloodsucking leech.

The dampened spirit escalated. Why do people in the same denomination have such different views on healing? I understand the differences between denominations, but I couldn't grasp why some people live as though miracles are a thing of the past.

I refrained from sharing my situation with Pastor Art. He was battling his own health crises, and shortly after my surgeries, he lost his fight with leukemia. Seems odd because I remember the multitude of times he encouraged me when I was in tears over Timmy's condition.

I found myself visiting a new app, Periscope. Restoring Hope Church streamed live services on the app. It was a new church in Hendersonville, Tennessee pastored by Aaron and Amanda Crabb. Periscope fell by the wayside once Facebook Live began, but it provided me with believers of like-minded faith. During their services, I chatted with someone at the church, along with others watching. Sort of an online church, which isn't a substitute for church, but sadly, sometimes it's all we have. They always believed my eyes would be healed. I cultivated new friendships there.

One evening, I spoke with a preacher and his wife who were visiting our church. Surely they would believe and cover me in prayer, so I described the wondrous ways God had shown me He was going to improve my vision. You could have heard a pin drop. Their speechless response shocked me. Yes, they would pray for me, but I could feel their doubts.

Friday night took forever to roll around. Jason Crabb was in concert at a church nearby. Excitement filled my heart. Hope and encouragement surrounded me at this concert. Jason sang a song from his new CD called "Chance for a Miracle." He asked the crowd, "Does anyone need a miracle tonight?"

My hand shot up, as I praised God along with many others seeking an answer to their own dilemmas.

I had a few minutes to talk to Jason during intermission. He remembered praying for my vision at the Gatlinburg Gathering, one month earlier. He asked how things were going. I described how people were bringing me down. He told me to let them be discouraged, but don't let them discourage me.

Jason gave an altar call, and a crowd gathered. Then Jason asked the entire church to pray concerning my surgery. I will never forget the sound of three hundred-plus people saying "Amen."

Three years later, I see with some improvement in vision, and I also see the wisdom in Jason's advice. Our job isn't to transform people from doubting Thomases into people of strong faith. We can share what the Bible says and the multiple times we are commanded to trust God to answer our prayers. If they prefer to live in negativity, let them. Our duty is to prevent them from swaying us from a firm faith.

This world is a trying place for Christians to survive without the constant berating from others. The ultimate way to handle these folks is to keep our distance from them. But what if that's an impossibility? What if they are in church with us? On our jobs? In our families? Words of dismay must fall on deaf ears.

"Even on a rainy day, the Son still shines." - Author unknown

Perhaps you are down in the dumps due to the circumstances of life, not people. You never get a break. Everywhere you turn, trouble follows you. You try harder, but nothing turns out right. A constant dripping wears you thin.

Whatever the source of your discouragement, we are not without hope. Believers have God's Holy Word, sixty-six books overflowing with faith. When we are unnerved by doom and gloom popping up in our lives, we must turn to this love letter from our heavenly Father.

The Psalms are rich with hope for the downtrodden. We can turn to our favorite promises. The promises that God provides. The promises that God gives us His strength. The promise that this world is the worst we will ever experience, and the glories awaiting us are beyond our greatest imagination.

We have access to the throne room 24/7, and our Father meets our needs with divine resources. He wants to carry our burdens and He tells us to unload them on Him. God wants to take every single one of them and free us from the heavy loads.

We are not alone in the battle for encouragement. Abraham faced it when he remained childless for twenty-five years. Noah dealt with it while he labored over the ark. David grappled with it when Saul hunted him down. Paul wrestled with it when he was imprisoned. When he was beaten. When he was ship-wrecked. Hope exists!

Let's examine what the Bible says. Despair is derived from three sources: the devil, people, and our situations.

Even though people and circumstances bring us down, the true source behind them is our enemy. We get a special glimpse into heaven in Job chapter one when Satan and God discuss righteous Job. During this encounter, we discover that Satan must obtain permission from God to touch a Christian. He wants to afflict God's children hoping to create torment and destroy our faith. It's safe to say that in the following two cases, the devil is behind the scenes.

An example of hopelessness spread by people is in Numbers chapters thirteen and fourteen. Upon reaching the promised land, Moses sent out twelve spies to report back on the condition of the land. An Old Testament version of a travel brochure. After spending forty days in the land flowing with milk and honey, they returned with a mixed report.

The men brought evidence of the land's goodness just as God had promised. A cluster of grapes so large that it took two men to carry them on a pole over their shoulders. Can you imagine finding that in Walmart? They also brought pomegranates and figs back to show the children of Israel.

Ten spies reported the land certainly flowed with milk and honey; nevertheless, the inhabitants looked strong. Too strong. They continued describing the fortified cities as large. These are the same voices we hear today. The voices of doubt.

Canaan is exactly as God said it would be, but... When you hear "but" or "nevertheless" you know it cannot be good news. Here comes the bad news, no matter what God has promised. These ten spies represented ten of the tribes of Israel, and their doubtful hearts also represented the attitude of the majority.

God, who had led them out of Egypt. God, who parted the Red Sea. God, who miraculously fed them manna and gave them water from a rock. God was right about the land, but the people feared God could not handle strong Canaanites.

Two spies trusted God, Joshua and Caleb. Anticipating the disbelief spreading through the camp, Caleb suggested they go up and take possession of the land immediately because Israel could overcome it. Caleb believed God. Joshua and Caleb are our heroes of faith. We admire them and desire similar qualities.

But the ten responded negatively, declaring they were unable to fight against the powerful Canaanites. They proceeded to give a bad report about the land, full of lies and exaggerations. Compared to the giants of Canaan, they felt like grasshoppers.

Mission accomplished. Discouragement and doubt spread swiftly throughout the Israelites, and they withdrew from the plans to possess the Promised Land. They complained about their leaders, Moses and Aaron. They wished they had remained in Egypt as slaves. They even grumbled about God bringing them to such a dismal place.

Moses and Aaron began to pray, interceding on behalf of the people. Meanwhile, Joshua and Caleb tried convincing the Israelites that refusing to enter the land was an act of rebellion toward God. Joshua and Caleb explained that God would give them victory, but you cannot force people to believe. Their faith isn't weak or small. They were faithless, and that faithlessness kept them in the wilderness for almost another forty years. Just like fear and worry, doubt cannot coexist with faith. Is that statement too strong? Not when we consider God's reaction to the lack of faith in the Israelite camp.

God told Moses He would strike them with a pestilence and disinherit them. Was God really planning to afflict His chosen people? Yes, because they failed to trust Him. Lack of faith disrespects God. It denies His character because God is faithful. We can rely on God and His promises.

Moses begged God for mercy on Israel. His motive had absolutely nothing to do with the doubtful multitude. If God failed to deliver the Israelites to the promised land, the other nations would mock God. Moses couldn't risk God's name being disgraced, and God heard the prayer of Moses and pardoned Israel.

God's response to unbelief provides insight into the dangers that accompany disheartenment. We never want to be the voice of negativity. We want to speak the Word and its truths. Believers are lights in a dark world. When a brother or sister feels low, we help lift them up and strengthen them in their faith.

We must tread cautiously around people spreading the spirit of hopelessness. Guard your faith so no one removes your confidence in the Lord.

Now let's look at a daunting situation. We traverse these frequently. Like people, they can bring us down before we realize our faith is waning.

In 1 Kings chapter 17, Elijah proclaimed a drought. The Lord instructed Elijah to depart and turn east toward the brook Cherith, where the Lord provided for him. Elijah drank from the waters of the brook, and ravens brought him bread and meat every morning and evening.

After some time without rain, the brook dried up. God instructed him to go to Zarephath. The Lord told Elijah He had commanded a widow there to provide for him.

Elijah may have wondered how a poor widow would be able to provide for him, but as a prophet of God, He trusted the Lord.

At the city gate, Elijah found a widow gathering sticks. He politely asked her for a cup of water. She turned to get the water, and Elijah asked for a morsel of bread. Remember, God told Elijah He had commanded this widow to provide for him.

But the widow admitted to Elijah that she had no bread, only a little flour and oil. What? Isn't this the widow the Lord commanded to provide for Elijah? Her next statement might have made Elijah reconsider if he had the correct widow. She said she was going to prepare her last bit of flour and oil for her and her son. They would eat it and die.

OK, I would definitely be questioning God now. Did she hear You right, Lord? You said she would provide for me. My thoughts, not Elijah's.

Elijah calmly told the widow not to fear. He told her to make her food, but she must make him a small cake first. Afterward, she could make the remainder for her and her son. Elijah says,

"For thus says the Lord God of Israel: 'The bin of flour shall not be used up, nor shall the jar of oil run dry, until the day the Lord sends rain on the earth." (1 Kings 17:14)

The widow obeyed the prophet's words. The bin of flour and the oil never ran dry, and they ate for many days. This was an encouraging outcome for both the widow and Elijah. But then the boy died.

The widow's blood began to boil, and she seemed to blame Elijah for her son's death. Elijah carried the boy upstairs and he cried out to the Lord. Now, if ever, Elijah felt unnerved, because he asked God why He killed the boy.

Elijah stretched himself out on the widow's son and prayed for healing. The Lord didn't speak to Elijah, but He answered Elijah's prayer.

The widow and Elijah were overjoyed, and finally, she declared she knew Elijah was sent from God. Elijah may have sensed some defeat slipping in at times, but the widow was beaten down from the beginning.

Life hadn't been kind in quite some time. How often do you meet someone who plans to eat their last meal and die, excluding death row? Their life had been a struggle for many seasons. Maybe even before her husband passed from this world. She tried being both mother and father to this boy. She wanted to give him better than she could afford. The drought in the land had increased her hardships. She carried around a tremendous burden. Yet, something inspired her to feed Elijah. Perhaps she figured she had nothing to lose, or was it the voice of the Lord?

Listen to the voice of Christ. Mute the voice of the crisis.

But when her son died, her doubts intensified. She might have second-guessed her decision to allow Elijah to stick around. Distrust had been in her heart all along. After God revived her son, she professed that Elijah truly was a man of God (1 Kings 17:24).

Friend, we aren't conquering strong nations like the Israelites, but we live in a world where people spread unbelief. The type of unbelief that causes us to doubt God. Doubt that makes it hard to firmly believe God will remain faithful. You may be facing something today, and as you claim God's promise, a dispenser of misery tells you how unrealistic your hopes are. Don't allow them to dash your faith in the Lord. Don't allow them to steal your belief for healing. Don't fall for the lies that God won't make a way. Don't listen to the voice that says it is useless to keep serving the Lord. Believe addictions can be overcome. Believe the prodigals will return. Believe chains can be broken, and hearts can be mended.

Perhaps you can relate to the widow. Life has given you lemons, but you don't have any sugar to make lemonade. One thing after another chisels away at you. A repair. A bill. A diagnosis. Another repair. Friend, I have been there, and these burdens always come in groups. Sometimes, the picture of doom and gloom is painted so drably that we make the decision not to venture out into what God wants us to do. Possibly missing out on something wonderful God had in store.

Last year, God led me to make a big decision. Change denominations and churches. It wasn't my decision because God directed me. I took my time, not rushing into it. I asked God for several confirmations.

My word for 2018 was faith, and it required a giant step of faith to make this change. It didn't take long for me to realize how much I needed this pastor and congregation.

I am at the altar every Sunday. My faith constantly increases, and my relationship with the Lord runs deeper. I have experienced healings and breakthroughs. I am with people who love, accept, and support me like I have never experienced before.

A few people tried to sway my decision, but I listened to God. Just like the Israelites should have done. Look at the multiple blessings I would have missed if I had allowed negativity to have a voice. My church family at New Life Fellowship is a rare commodity. Money can't buy it. I love them bunches.

If discouragement surrounds us, how do we overcome it? What do we do when we can't take anymore? How do we handle all the pessimism?

When the world weighs us down, God will raise us up.

But those who wait on the Lord
Shall renew their *strength;*
They shall mount up with wings like eagles
They shall run and not be weary,
They shall walk and not faint. (Isaiah 40:31)

Wait on the Lord. Naysayers and unfavorable conditions surround us, not to mention Old Slew Foot. We must possess the sweet fruit of the Holy Spirit, patience. Like stability, patience is a reoccurring quality necessary for strong faith. We may need to endure some things, for some time. Even an extremely long time. So, we wait on the Lord. We do as He has directed until He tells us to do the next thing.

Sometimes, we wait for the truth to be revealed. I am guilty of getting down in the dumps when I fail to see the whole picture. I could peacefully wait to see how all the pieces of the puzzle fit together. Instead, I rush into the worst-case scenario.

Always remember God is busy on our behalf even though it appears as if nothing is happening. He goes before us, preparing the way.

Many times, God enlists us to stay busy. This is not impatiently jumping in and doing what we think is best. God's children aren't sitting in a heavenly waiting room bored out of our minds, reading magazines until our name is called. Instead, God gives us work to accomplish.

While we wait, we trust. When we have a firm, unshakable confidence that God is going to intervene at His proper time, we will be filled with peace.

Waiting without trusting is wrestling.

But when we trust in the Lord, our wait is peaceful. Jesus never promised this world would be easy. Actually, He said the opposite:

"These things I have spoken to you, that in Me you may have peace. In the world you will have tribulation; but be of good cheer, I have overcome the world." (John 16:33)

When trouble arises, we cry out to Jesus. and we trust His plan.

As we continue unpacking our verse, we learn that God renews our strength. We need fresh strength because the world and the devil have beaten us down. In the same manner that our cars need to be refueled at the gas pumps, our strength needs a boost. God infuses us with His mighty strength, enabling us to do anything (Philippians 4:13).

Now, we arrive at my favorite part of this verse. We must learn some things about eagles to grasp the fullness of what Isaiah is saying. Eagles have a wingspan averaging about seven feet. Eagles can carry large bodies of prey while flying. They can fly at speeds up to forty miles per hour. Impressive.

Although these majestic birds are extremely capable, they rely on a force other than themselves. Instead of exerting their energy, they sail along on air currents.

How often do we feel inadequate? We don't retain the fortitude to continue, but God does. He wants us to depend on Him in the same way the eagles depend on air currents.

According to eagleflight.org, the eagles carry their young on their wings. This is part of the baby eaglet's flying lessons. Momma eagle knocks baby eagle out of its warm, comfy nest. All the security the eaglet has ever known is swept out from under him. Then, momma eagle swoops down to catch him on her wings, carrying him back to the nest.

We wait on the Lord. Strength is refueled, and we shall mount up with wings like eagles.

As if we were riding on the wings of an eagle, God will swoop in and carry us above our bleak circumstances. We will soar over our problems. High above the discouragement. All the misery of the world will seem myopic when God is our focus.

God will enable us to run the race without weariness. That new jolt of strength will give us the endurance to not only run, but to finish. Life can be wearisome. God invigorates us with everything necessary to survive it all.

Finally, we will walk without fainting. We will not tire out. On this journey of faith, God will supply us with the energy, the grace, and the power to finish. We will not faint by the wayside.

While we wait on God, we wait with God.

The battle between encouragement and discouragement occurs in our minds, just like fear and worry. A mind centered on God sees hope on the horizon. Clearly, keeping our thoughts God-centered is half the battle. Godly thoughts say, "I can" rather than "I can't."

Defeating discouragement silences the lies.

The lies of the devil (the father of lies). Lies from our flesh. Lies from the doom and gloom crowd. Lies of unbelief. We can speak the truth, the Word of God, which has the power to slay all lies.

Can you imagine where we will be when we banish discouragement from our lives? We will be victors, no longer victims. Think about the healthy disposition we will possess. People will wonder in amazement why we are so upbeat. The joy in our hearts will shine on our faces.

Finally, consider the encouragement we can provide to others. We won't be like the ten spies who brought the bad news back to the Israelites. No, we will be like Joshua and Caleb, full of enthusiasm about what God has in store.

Discouragement is contagious, but encouragement is victorious.

Friend, we are victorious children of the King. The King who is faithful to His promises. The King whom we trust. We have grasped the abundant life He offered us. We have risen above the storm clouds, and we will mount up like eagles, soaring high, far above it all.

Lord, we desire to sail upon Your wings above all the misgivings below. Lift our hearts and spirits. Help us trust wholeheartedly in You. In Jesus' name, Amen.

Stepping Stones

When the world weighs us down, God will raise us up.

Listen to the voice of Christ. Mute the voice of the crisis.

Waiting without trusting is wrestling.

While we wait on God, we wait with God.

Defeating discouragement silences the lies.

Discouragement is contagious, but encouragement is victorious.

Scripture

But those who wait on the Lord
Shall renew their strength;
They shall mount up with wings like eagles
They shall run and not be weary,
They shall walk and not faint. (Isaiah 40:31)

These things I have spoken to you, that in Me you may have peace. In the world you will have tribulation; but be of good cheer, I have overcome the world. (John 16:33)

CHAPTER 8

LIVING ON EMPTY

I leaned against my little girl's empty dresser with tears streaming. I slumped down onto the floor. Hugging my knees, I decided to end my life since God hadn't answered my cries for relief.

God and Satan were playing tug-of-war with me. I was being torn in two directions.

"Take the pills! You have enough to do it."

"No, this misery will pass. I am with you. If you do this, she wins."

Have you ever felt pain so relentless you questioned whether you would survive? Has sorrow cut to the depths of your heart? Have your burdens crushed you under their weight?

The darkest times of our lives will require more than ignoring emotions. We choose to trust God, but no relief emerges on the horizon.

Clinical depression bound me with heavy, seemingly unbreakable chains for weeks. When would the suffering end? God, please make it end!

Day after day, tears escaped unceasingly. Anything and everything produced an emotional avalanche. I picked over my food with no real interest, except for sweets. I gorged on them begging them to numb the pain. Nothing beckoned to me. No interest in any activity. Life held no attraction either. It became a horrific task I had to endure until it ended, and I begged God to take me home.

When I found the luxury of sleep, I dreaded the moment I awoke. Each time I did, I had to relive the nightmare of my life.

I had unintentionally penciled God out of my schedule that year. Actually, both times I survived depression, I had overextended myself. My world centered around my daughter. Little time remained for God between home school activities and making arrangements for my mom in a halfway decent nursing facility for dementia patients. Now, my mom didn't recognize me, and my daughter became the prodigal. Since she was eighteen, she could shun Jesus and Momma both, but it meant living elsewhere. Not only did she leave, she broke off all communication, like I explained in an earlier chapter.

Throughout my day, I floundered from one extreme to another. Life as I knew it, as I dreamt it, had ceased to exist. An eerie silence whispered through the house, replacing forgotten laughter and liveliness. Her footsteps no longer danced through the door. My empty nest shouted "abandoned."

Sadness swept in. I mourned her. Thank God, she was alive. Thank God, she could return, but it was mourning still the same.

I wonder if anger is the heart's self-defense mechanism. Anger numbs the anguish. It spared me from crying. She had betrayed me. I had devoted my life to her, helped her buy a car. I sacrificed time and effort to homeschool her. How could she walk out on me? Eighteen years of total devotion, and she ripped my heart out and stomped it.

I made an appointment with my doctor. He prescribed antidepressants. I felt an immediate change. I had more control over my feelings, which juggled between grief and betrayal.

After some time, I thought I could safely stop taking them under my doctor's supervision. Never do it on your own. You need to wean yourself off them. Stopping cold turkey often results in suicide attempts.

For years, I carried around a heart, not quite mended. Not having a relationship with your own flesh and blood feels unnatural at best and devastating at its worst. My friends' daughters graduated, attended college, got married, and had children. They had a family for Thanksgiving and Christmas. They gave birthday presents to their daughters, but I couldn't. They had mother-daughter shopping trips. Reminders of what I lost encircled me. How I wished I could share those activities with my daughter.

Nine years later, I traveled the same dark road. This time, I was in a much better relationship with the Lord, but I had bitten off more than I could chew. I was publishing my second book, *Incense Rising: 60 Days to Powerful Prayer*. After professional editing and formatting, it needed proofing. Something I cannot do myself with my visual impairment, so it became my husband's job. He had ten days to proof the entire manuscript. This caught me by surprise, because my first book had only been in a digital format. It hadn't required the same standards as a print book.

Timmy's brother, Matt, was at Duke Medical Center with a setback. He was awaiting a liver transplant. Timmy felt he needed to drive to North Carolina and check on Matt. His plan was to return the next day at the latest.

When he arrived, he found Matt on life support. The doctors urged Timmy to stay and make important decisions. I felt my husband's pain, and I tried to help. I kept preachers updated plus fed and watered Matt's dog.

I paid my editor to look over my book, since Timmy couldn't, but the news devastated me. She uncovered numerous mistakes at a glance. I emailed the list of corrections to my formatter, John. It shocked me when he corrected them and wanted this file proofed too. I couldn't continue paying for proofing. I refused to burden Timmy with this news. What was I going to do?

I felt like Moses as I declared to God that I couldn't proofread my work. How did God expect me, a blind woman, to write without the ability to proof my work? Between sobs, I complained about the unfairness of my situation.

"God, if You want this book published, bring my husband home. Do something! I can't do this alone!"

Moses had a speech impediment. I have a visual impairment. Why does God call broken vessels to serve Him? Why would He allow such hardships when I needed something to go right? Have you ever felt the disappointment when God doesn't work according to our plans? It's hard to wrap our minds around it.

Frustration overwhelmed me. I cried. Then I cried some more. Timmy was absent for days, and we had not prepared for any of this. I ran low on groceries. I ran out of toothpaste. It didn't help when I decided to play Super Blind Woman, ready to handle everything in a single bound.

I could do all of this! I could handle the dog. I would go online and buy toothpaste. I could take a cab and buy groceries.

Sounds great, but in 2016, I had never done any of these things independently. Not until Iva did I obtain this freedom.

I discovered Satan loves isolated victims. He cornered me and my book about prayer as he waged His attack. I have found that many people who battle depression keep it quiet. We become quite talented at wearing the mask with the big smile. If I am ever bound by those chains again, I hope to remember this:

Don't isolate, but gravitate.

Tell someone. Not those who judge, but a compassionate someone. We also need to gravitate toward the Son, like a sunflower.

Sunflowers earn their name because their blooms follow the sun. Sunflowers, like humans, possess an internal clock. They track the sun from east to west during the day. At night, they turn east to begin a new day.*

Depression is such a thick blackness that it interferes with our Son tracking. I buckled under the weight of everything going wrong. Feeling like a failure who could not attain any independence. The meltdown hit its climax when I didn't know which brand of toothpaste I used. I never realized the varieties of toothpaste on the market. Depression behaves like that. It obsesses over something trivial. Any toothpaste would work until Timmy returned, but Super Blind Woman had to get it right. I refused to ask anyone for help.

I felt broken as a person. I added to my own misery by setting the bar too high. Not accepting anything besides perfection. Like a car, I was running on empty. How had it come to this? Inadequacy, worthlessness, defeat, and rejection made their grand appearances. I considered ending it all to escape the pain. No matter how it affected anyone, I wanted the agony to cease.

My raw emotions stung with each floundering step of self-reliance. What worth was I? All I could do was look within, incapable of supporting my husband in his urgent hour of need. I failed to comfort him.

I recognized my symptoms. Depression. I realized I needed antidepressants again, but I couldn't get an appointment with my doctor until after the Memorial Day weekend. I dared not tell them I spent most of my day contemplating death. I wiped my schedule clean. I decided to let the book rest for a few days.

Honestly, after my daughter disappeared, I longed for heaven. Not that I constantly sought death, but this world held nothing but pain for me.

Loneliness invaded my world. I couldn't even sense God's presence. I cried out desperately seeking a word from heaven, but nothing. I should have leaned on Him sooner, but now He couldn't rescue me fast enough.

What was wrong with me? Had God abandoned me? I knew God never leaves us or forsakes us (Hebrews 13:5), but I felt His silence. God and I rarely had one-sided conversations, so this was abnormal. I stretched out on the lawn chair, warmed by the sun. I stared into heaven, and asked, "Where are You, God?"

There goes my ministry. Who wants to read a book by a basket case? Who would invite a hypocrite to speak? I am the encourager. I tell people they can survive anything, but now I was losing it. And over what? At that moment, I remembered a radio interview I had heard. She was well known in the Christian world, and she spoke openly about her depression. Sheila Walsh. My first glimmer of hope shined like a candle in the dark. I scrolled through her list of books on my phone until I found *Loved Back to Life.*

Immediately I began reading, amazed at the similarities in our symptoms. The selfishness, the pain, and yes, the inability to feel God by my side.

I realized I needed to continue taking antidepressants. Another similarity to Sheila's story. Too many times, I erupted into tears. Too many times, something brought me down.

Some of those dark days felt like life could never get better, like I was drowning in despair. If you are there now, I encourage you to get the help you need, medically and emotionally. And never stop leaning on Jesus. His specialty is broken hearts.

Perhaps you aren't drowning in depression, but you feel you can't keep your head above water. Someone has hurt you. Abandoned you. Abused you. Maybe they left this world too soon. Your family might be coming apart at the seams. Divorce, drugs, or drinking has destroyed them. Has disaster struck, leaving you with nothing? Has one moment in time changed the trajectory of your life? The life-altering accident. The baby who never made it home from the hospital. You thought your child-rearing years were over, and now you are raising grandkids. Are you caring for aging parents while your own health fails?

When life lets us down, it often resembles a multi-car accident on the highway. It's never just one problem. No, they continue to multiply. The devastating diagnosis leads to a mountain of bills. Nothing and no one seem reliable any longer. It is you against the world. But friend, you are not alone. You have Jesus. We have Jesus.

Before we turn from my darkness and your darkness into the light, let's examine the Bible's dark moments. Depression was prevalent in Scripture. David, Elijah, and Jonah were plagued with it. Jeremiah was known as the weeping prophet, and Job suffered great loss.

Even our Lord experienced deep affliction. He was called "a Man of sorrows and acquainted with grief" (Isaiah 53:3). In the garden of Gethsemane, we see His turmoil.

He began to be troubled and deeply distressed. Then He said to them, "My soul is exceedingly sorrowful, even to death."
(Mark 14:33b-34a)

Jesus agonized to the degree that His sweat became blood (Luke 22:44). My friend, if Jesus Christ, God the Son, could endure such grief, why do we feel ashamed when we are afflicted?

Despondency is sprinkled throughout the Psalms. David had an extremely dysfunctional family. His father refused to envision David on the throne. King David, a man after God's own heart and a giant-slaying warrior, traveled many roads of despair. We cannot consider ourselves weak when David suffered the same emotional sting. David penned these words:

My tears have been my food day and night,
While they continually say to me,
"Where is your God?"

When I remember these things,
I pour out my soul within me.
For I used to go with the multitude;
I went with them to the house of God,
With the voice of joy and praise,
With a multitude that kept a pilgrim feast.

Why are you cast down, O my soul?
And why are you disquieted within me?
Hope in God, for I shall yet praise Him
For the help of His countenance. (Psalm 42:3-5)

David sat down with his feelings. Turning towards them, he asked, "Why are you so down?" Then David allowed his faith to speak: "Hope in God." David won the battle when he declared he would praise God. That's what we must do, friend.

Allow our faith to speak to our feelings.

Faith has scared my fears off. It's calmed worry, but corralling extreme emotions is challenging. Let's visit a woman in 2 Kings chapter four. She was living on empty. Her husband had passed away at an early age, leaving her with two sons to raise alone. Even though he had been a son of the prophets and a blessed servant of God, he was taken away from her prematurely.

None of us are immune to crises. No matter how obediently we live. No matter how sanctified we become. No matter how deep we trust, tribulations visit all of us.

This nameless widow ached for her husband. She fell asleep recalling how he embraced her on cold nights, only to awaken to the reminder of his absence. She missed the instruction he rendered the boys and his spiritual leadership in the home. Her heart broke with grief, but her heart wasn't the only thing broken.

Her finances had been spent. Perhaps debt existed before her husband died. Being a prophet wasn't a wealthy occupation, and persecution against men of God spread throughout the land.

The debt collector would settle her debt at the expense of her sons. It was the custom as well as part of the Mosaic law for young men to exchange seven years of service as bondservants in order to cancel debts.

Still mourning her husband, the devastation of losing her boys loomed over her. The widow had sold all their earthly goods, but she still fell short. She explained her plight to Elijah, reminding him of her husband's service. He asked her what remained in the house. She owned nothing but a small jar of oil.

When life crumbles around us, don't we feel empty? Often, we neglect to see what is right before our eyes. We focus on our lack, not our blessings.

With both rounds of depression, I did that. I had lost my daughter, but I had a loving husband who did everything to get me through that horrible ordeal. I had my health and my home. We had an income, but I stared at the empty bedroom.

Stare at what is instead of what isn't.

Now, Elijah told our widow to do something illogical.

Then he said, "Go, borrow vessels from everywhere, from all your neighbors—empty vessels; do not gather just a few." (2 Kings 4:3)

The prophet's widow knew better than to argue with Elijah. God works in ways man cannot comprehend. The woman and her two sons went door-to-door borrowing as many empty vessels as possible. Can you imagine the inquisitiveness from her friends? What a testimony of faith this family was about to become. Remember Elijah's final command to her? Don't only collect a few. The vessels she collected were in proportion to her faith. A doubter would think the whole idea foolish and only collect several bowls. Eyes of faith would gather as many jars, bowls, pots, and pans as possible.

It helped this poor woman to get out of the house. Many times, life's interruptions and disappointments cause us to isolate ourselves. What better way to have a pity party than in solitude? Of course, Satan crashes our party and reinforces our negative thoughts.

Our widow had some much-needed social time, and now she was ready for part two of Elijah's plan.

"And when you have come in, you shall shut the door behind you and your sons; then pour it into all those vessels, and set aside the full ones."

So she went from him and shut the door behind her and her sons, who brought the vessels to her; and she poured it out.

Now it came to pass, when the vessels were full, that she said to her son, "Bring me another vessel."

And he said to her, "There is not another vessel." So the oil ceased.

Then she came and told the man of God. And he said, "Go, sell the oil and pay your debt; and you and your sons live on the rest."
(2 Kings 4:4-7)

The widow and her boys went behind closed doors and began to pour out the oil into all the empty vessels. God doesn't put His miracles on display like a performance. They are reserved for eyes of faith. That original little bottle of oil kept reproducing each time it was poured out. God multiplied the oil until the last vessel was full. Hence the necessity for gathering many bowls and the capacity for much faith.

She had enough oil to sell and pay off her debt, plus, she had her retirement fund. God provided this family with suitable means of living for the rest of her life.

God didn't just hand her a blank check. No, He made her get out and be part of the solution. When she placed her gaze from what she lacked to what she possessed, she gained a new perspective.

The anointing abides!

As I studied this passage, God revealed something. The oil remained. The anointing remained. Although some commentators suggest this was cooking oil, most of them believe it was anointing oil. Anointing oil had a higher value. Like the Holy Spirit's anointing, which is priceless.

Several weeks ago, some people noticed Iva, my usually beautiful shiny black Lab, had some dandruff. I posted in one of the guide dog Facebook groups about my flaky situation. As I expected, Iva's problem was shared by other Labs. One lady noted it occurred each year when they turn on the heat. Bingo. That was when it happened. She suggested a teaspoon of olive oil in Iva's food daily.

Water and oil don't mix, so I added the oil to her food before I added water. When she finished, she kept licking the bottom of the bowl like she couldn't get enough of the flavor.

Upon examining the seemingly clean bowl, I felt the oil in the bottom. I had poured oil on the food. Only one teaspoon. I had mixed it. I had added water and stirred.

The oil remained! Friend, our anointing remains! No matter what drains us of everything else, the power of God sticks with us.

Disease can ravage our bodies, but the anointing remains. Finances fizzle out, but the anointing remains. Misery can mess with our minds, but the anointing remains. People leave us, but the anointing remains.

I discovered something else about the anointing when I had emptied myself of everything. The anointing heals. Six weeks after my daughter left, I chose to stop grieving. This was a decision I made in spite of my sorrow. During a Sunday night service, I felt God move me toward the altar. The sermon spoke straight to my aching soul. God moved me on with life. Pastor Art preached on the words of David:

Weeping may endure for a night, but joy comes *in the morning.* (Psalm 30:5b)

After eight years of silence, I heard from my daughter. It wasn't the prodigal returning home. She showed no regret for her previous actions, and now another hurdle existed. My daughter was a homosexual.

I loved her. I reiterated that God loved her, but He didn't love her sin. It remains a stormy relationship.

Friend, if I survived depression, I know with the Lord you can survive anything. He came to give us the oil of joy for mourning (Isaiah 61:3). He gives us the garment of praise for the spirit of heaviness. Weeping comes for a night, and maybe another night, but joy comes in the morning.

I want to share another passage of Scripture. Paul, like us, endured seasons of despair, disaster, and deep disappointment. He wrote:

...that we were burdened beyond measure, above strength, so that we despaired even of life. Yes, we had the sentence of death in ourselves, that we should not trust in ourselves but in God who raises the dead, who delivered us from so great a death, and does deliver us; in whom we trust that He will still deliver us, (2 Corinthians 1:8c-10)

You have carried those immeasurable burdens. Paul suffered differently than I, and your hardships differ from mine. Yet, we all share in the weakness and hopelessness that accompany trouble.

We can hold tight to God's promise of deliverance. When we fall into despair. When death seems inevitable, whether it is the death of a loved one, a marriage, or a relationship. Even when life is desperately painful, and we seek death.

When we are overburdened, overloaded, and overwhelmed, God overcomes.

His resurrection power raises dead marriages. It turns burdens into blessings. It heals and strengthens.

But let's not jump too far ahead. That's just a snapshot of your future. For now, you're going to stop living on empty, and fill up your faith tank. Today, you still hurt. Today, you still don't know where life leads. Today, you pray. Claim His promises. When there's nothing left for you to give, you've made room for God.

Dark valleys are inescapable, but God makes us capable.

Trials don't come to hurt us, but to help us. To heal us. The widow got down to nothing. Paul despaired unto death. I experienced an emotional tsunami. God didn't allow these things for harm, but for our good and His glory. In each case, the anointing abided. The power of God on our lives survived. The resurrection power dwelling in us continues.

When we beg God to bring our crises to a screeching halt, we are actually grieving the Holy Spirit. Our complaining quenches the Holy Spirit, because the struggle helps us. Dr. Tony Evans tells the story about the metamorphosis of a caterpillar. The struggle to break out of the cocoon develops the butterfly's strong wings.

Sweet friend, in your striving today, God is developing your strength and transforming you into a mighty Christian soldier. Dwell in that cocoon until God completes His transforming work. When you live on empty, room remains for the anointing.

Whatever darkness ensnares you today, hold on to this truth:

Trials don't come to hurt me, but to help me.

Allow God to have His perfect work. Choose faith. Refuse to allow emotions to hold you hostage. Give God your emptiness and ask Him to feel you with His power. His Holy Spirit. His anointing. Then you can rule over your feelings, rather than your feelings ruling over you.

Heavenly Father, we know without a doubt that You can speak a word and change everything. Lord, I want Your will in my life, whatever You desire to accomplish. You have all of me, not a fraction. Not a portion. Let Your anointing fall from heaven and fill me to the brim. In Jesus' name, Amen.

Stepping Stones

Don't isolate, but gravitate.

Allow our faith to speak to our feelings.

The anointing abides!

Stare at what is instead of what isn't.

When we are overburdened, overloaded, and overwhelmed, God overcomes.

Dark valleys are inescapable, but God makes us capable.

Trials don't come to hurt me, but to help me.

You can rule over your feelings, rather than your feelings ruling over you.

Scripture

My tears have been my food day and night,
While they continually say to me,
"Where is your God?"

When I remember these things,
I pour out my soul within me.
For I used to go with the multitude;
I went with them to the house of God,
With the voice of joy and praise,
With a multitude that kept a pilgrim feast.

Why are you cast down, O my soul?
And why are you disquieted within me?
Hope in God, for I shall yet praise Him
For *the help of His countenance.* (Psalm 42:3-5)

Weeping may endure for a night, but joy comes in the morning.
(Psalm 30:5b)

...that we were burdened beyond measure, above strength, so that we despaired even of life. Yes, we had the sentence of death in ourselves, that we should not trust in ourselves but in God who raises the dead, who delivered us from so great a death, and does deliver us; in whom we trust that He will still deliver us, (2 Corinthians 1:8c-10)

- https://www.npr.org/sections/thetwo-way/2016/08/05/488891151/the-mystery-of-why-sunflowers-turn-to-follow-the-sun-solved

PART III

PRAYER THAT PREVAILS

CHAPTER 9

ABIDING IN ABUNDANCE

Frustration hit its boiling point. I had prayed that morning. Then I prayed before my braille class, but now I wanted to scream and throw the book on the floor, smashing all those dots. Which letter of the alphabet was eluding me now?

"God, I need Your grace, and I need it now! I cannot do this without You."

When grace rushes in, frustration rushes out.

That ritual played out almost every braille lesson. It was the hardest part of rehabilitation.

My vision loss began at the early age of seven. While doing my second-grade homework, my mom asked me why I was holding my book so close to my eyes. I shrugged my shoulders. I hadn't noticed anything different. The journey to multiple doctors and diagnoses began. For years, I never knew all the names the doctors used to label my condition. Macular degeneration claimed the top spot in 2010.

My vision crept away, slowly. All through school, I read large-print books when available. In high school, they became scarce depending on the subject. I used regular-print textbooks with a high-powered magnifying glass when I was alone. I never could muster up the courage to use it in class. I idled away many hours at school pretending to read. After school, safe within the confines of my bedroom, I completed my assignment.

I tried faking normal vision around my peers, hoping to fit in. In my teens, I looked at menu boards as if I were making a choice, and then I ordered the same item every time.

In my twenties, reading became more difficult, and I began using a CCTV (closed-circuit television). It resembled a computer monitor, but it contained a camera that magnified printed or handwritten material on the screen. The CCTV has a wide range of magnification levels making myopic print readable. It also became the means by which I wrote out checks, letters, or envelopes. For years, this was the only way I could see the written word. Nowhere but home. Nowhere but in that chair, at my desk. Numerous times, I wished I could engross myself in a book while sitting in a waiting room, riding in the car, or relaxing on the beach. When Apple introduced the iPhone with Siri and VoiceOver, life improved for thousands of visually impaired people. Now I can enjoy books, study my Bible, send emails, and check Facebook anywhere, like sighted folks.

In 2010, my ophthalmologist gave me some encouraging news. My vision had reached a plateau. What a relief! Those were his last words to me, since he passed away several months later.

Medical advances in macular degeneration made it an exciting time to visit a new doctor. Dr. Myers' office transferred my records to Dr. White (fake name), but he couldn't locate them during my initial appointment. Dr. White spent only a few minutes with me. Within that short window of time, he diagnosed me with RP (retinitis pigmentosa). He explained that both disorders, RP and macular degeneration, along with cataracts, were plaguing my ability to see. He assured me my vision would never get worse.

Sitting in the exam chair, my mind raced back to someone with RP. I had researched it, and I remembered RP results in total blindness. I questioned Dr. White as my vision grew blurry from the dilation drops. Dr. White assured me my type of RP was different while he scribbled on a pad the name and amount of vitamin A he wanted me to take daily.

Later, I discovered a proper diagnosis of RP requires several specific tests. Dr. White never performed those tests. He couldn't even administer them in his office because they were only available at a nearby university hospital.

Vitamin A retinol proved impossible to find in the high doses he recommended. As Timmy and I searched, we discovered some warnings about taking large amounts of it. I found a multivitamin with a smaller amount. I began taking it daily, feeling less was the safer route.

I needed to increase the magnification on my CCTV—a red flag I ignored. No reason for concern since my vision had stabilized. Eventually, I began wondering why my vision was getting worse? Why was the decline more rapid than before?

Getting a driver's license had never been a possibility, so I walked everywhere. After Timmy and I were married, walking became a hobby. That all ended with an abrupt halt as my body hit a parked truck one day. The reality that I missed something that large rattled me. What if the next vehicle wasn't parked, but moving?

I had received some mobility training using a white cane from the Virginia Department for the Blind and Vision Impaired (DBVI) in recent years. The cane stayed in my closet. My daughter was ashamed for me to use it, but she wasn't alone. Old habits die hard, probably stemming from the teasing in school. One Sunday morning, at church, I bumped into a friend, almost knocking her down. I felt horrible, but I didn't explain that I never saw her. I wasn't ready to say those words.

Distinguishing between colors became a struggle, especially doing laundry. Sometimes, my clothes ended up in Timmy's closet. Despite what the doctors had said, I feared the onset of total blindness.

One of our favorite traditions was spending part of the Christmas season at Dollywood in Pigeon Forge, but two years had passed since our last trip there. After Christmas Day, we decided to finish out 2011 there. Memories enthused me as I packed. Millions of tiny lights sparkled across trees, buildings, and rides. Christmas melodies rang out as we strolled through the winter wonderland. Delicious hot chocolate chased away the chill as a blend of cedar and cinnamon filled the air.

We entered the gates, excited to greet the memorable illumination blanketing this Christmas village. We walked into a sea of people. Disappointment and shock enveloped me. This wasn't what I expected. Where were all the lights? Had they cut back? I clung to the back of Timmy's coat as we wiggled our way through bumper-to-bumper people.

When we reached a quieter place, I asked Timmy if Dollywood had made changes to the lighting. No, everything was the same. Timmy suggested that the crowd made it appear different to me. We had never been there in such a large crowd before.

We stepped into a warm theatre. When the show began, a bolt of truth struck me. I couldn't see most of the stage. Tears tried to escape, but I restrained them.

After an evening facing an abrupt reality, we bought subs and drove to our hotel. As we sat around the table in our room, I blurted out the truth. "I am going blind."

God healed Timmy's leukemia. He gave me boundless grace with my wayward child. Surely, He would see me through this.

Remember what God has done. Ask Him to do it again.

I contacted a specialist at Johns Hopkins Wilmer Eye Institute. Dr. Myers had referred me to them several years earlier. This specialist was conducting a clinical trial for a pill that might halt the vision loss. Once a patient's vision stabilized, they were placing new stem cells in the eyes, with some improvement.

Upon making an appointment, he conveyed one vital message via phone: No more vitamin A. He couldn't confirm that vitamin A robbed me of my vision, but enough evidence existed to support the fact that it does more damage than good in particular eye disorders.

After the initial visit, we made several trips to Johns Hopkins for additional testing. These tests led to another diagnosis: rod-cone dystrophy, a rare and genetic form of blindness. The clinical trial didn't begin until November, so I waited.

I trusted God's plan, but the unknown created some angsts. Whether you are losing your eyesight, your hearing, your arm, or leg, you are losing a significant part of life as you know it. It is human to dread an unknown future.

I made two lists of questions for the DBVI counselor's initial visit. One consisted of immediate concerns: pouring liquids in a glass, flipping a hamburger successfully, and safe mobility. The other list focused on the future: paperwork for my rental units, and my Bible study. Linda, my counselor and braille teacher, answered all my questions that first day. Getting answers and realizing a way exists to do everything calmed my nerves.

My rehab process began with braille. Braille comes in handy around the house for labeling items such as canned goods and CDs. Braille was the most problematic part of rehab. Imagine six positions, two dots wide and three dots tall, all of which fit under your fingertip. The letter or set of letters is determined by which positions the dots occupy, and memorizing it.

DBVI counselors warned me that rehab would be challenging. I bathed it in prayer, and I sought prayer from others for the difficult days ahead. I could only do this with God's help.

Life can never take us where grace will never find us.

I leaned on one of God's precious promises through this season:

I can do all things through Christ who strengthens me.
(Philippians 4:13)

Dramatic vision loss turned into a life-altering journey. When I drew near Jesus, and I trusted solely in Him to do anything and everything, I began walking in the deep waters of faith. As physical eyes dimmed, eyes of faith developed. I watched in wonder as God answered small requests, like finding something I misplaced. Amidst all the incredible things I can do through God's strength, the small things still matter to Him.

The protective hand of God has guided me around obstacles I never saw. Things I learned about afterward. I praise Him for safety, something we all take for granted. It is the times I discover what God has shielded me from that astound me.

During this season of my life, God called me to begin writing. It began with Christian devotionals to encourage people during their trials. I couldn't remain silent about the power of God when we rely confidently on Him.

Finally, the day arrived to return to Johns Hopkins. Some final tests would determine whether I could participate in the clinical trial.

We stopped at a small, isolated rest area. A Mennonite woman entered the bathroom as I was searching for the soap pump. She directed my hand towards it. She began talking about a blind friend as she handed me a paper towel. He owned a business and he could ride along with any of his employees and give them turn-by-turn directions. God could work like that in my life too. He had already begun.

When I reached the car, I almost told Timmy to turn around and go home. I wasn't going to be eligible for the trial. I knew it, and once we saw my doctor, he verified what God had already revealed.

Disappointment shadowed me for a short time. I wasn't shocked, though. My prayers were for God's will, not my selfish will. All along the prayer was for God to mold me into someone He could use. A willing vessel.

Sometimes Jesus heals, and sometimes He helps.

I have seen both sides, and the helping hand of our Lord provided me with a closer walk with Him. I adjusted to sight loss with God's grace. Eyesight is nice, but not necessary. I consider my vision loss a privilege, because it is an honor to walk this road with my Heavenly Father, taking each step of faith, holding His hand.

Seven years later, I see a multitude of times when God has received glory through my disability. That makes it all worthwhile.

His glory for His grace. His grace for His glory.

Friend, are you overwhelmed? Possibly an illness? Financial woes? Relationships in dire need of divine intervention? Depression? Grief? Heartache? Brokenness?

You feel defeated, and you wonder why. Why is this happening? Why hasn't God healed? Why hasn't God answered my prayers?

The Bible gives us clear instruction about answered prayer. I call them the ABCs of answered prayer. A is for abiding in Christ. B is for believing. C stands for committing our way to Him, and D is for delighting in the Lord. Let's look at a passage about abiding in the vine.

"I am the true vine, and My Father is the vinedresser. Every branch in Me that does not bear fruit He takes away; and every branch that bears fruit He prunes, that it may bear more fruit."
(John 15:1-2)

Since abiding in Christ empowers us to the degree that our prayers will be answered, we must understand what abiding in Christ entails. John chapter fifteen begins with one of the seven "I AM" statements. Jesus is the vine. God is the vinedresser or gardener. Matthew Henry considers Jesus as the root that dispenses its life-giving sap to the branches.

Believers are the branches, but we read about two types of branches: the fruit-bearing branches and the branches with absolutely no fruit.

Most commentators define the fruit-bearing branches as genuine Christians. The nonproductive ones are people professing to be believers, but they haven't experienced any real conversion. They have religion, but not the relationship.

I say this with love: The first step to abiding in Christ is to ensure you are born again. Check up on your salvation. Don't cling to some long-ago prayer or profession. Is there evidence that you have a personal relationship with Christ? Could a judge convict you of being a Christian?

Now, this is the part we don't like. God prunes the fruit-bearing branches. It doesn't matter how much fruit they bear, they all get pruned.

If you have ever pruned a shrub, you know it involves cutting, and while that creates no pain for your shrubs, the pruning process in the lives of believers hurts. Pruning eliminates areas of overgrowth and deadness. The first time I pruned my rhododendrons, I was amazed the following year when they greeted me with a sea of purple blooms. Plus, they experienced rapid growth. The same result occurs when God takes His pruning shears to us. Our fruit increases.

In this passage, Jesus spoke with the eleven disciples (Judas had departed.) He knew the difficulties they would face. First, His arrest and trial. Then His crucifixion and burial. Their faith would undergo its greatest test. Jesus considered all of this as He spoke about pruning.

Jesus could have miraculously taken His apostles with Him, but they had work to do on earth. They needed to be productive, and pruning brings about productivity. Less of them. More of Jesus.

The disciples were familiar with the grape vine. In order for a grapevine to bear more fruit, its branches must be cut back annually. Otherwise, the branches become woody, and the result is more branch than grapes. A grapevine with more vegetation doesn't produce more fruit. It bears less fruit.*

Less of the branches. More of the vine. Less of the disciples. More of Jesus. Less of me. More of Jesus. You get the idea.

When God saves us, He doesn't transport us to heaven. He leaves us here to produce fruit. Spreading the gospel, edifying the church, abounding in the fruits of the Spirit, loving others, and being constant in prayer.

What does the pruning process look like? It is any trial or hardship we endure, and as you can imagine, pruning hurts. The illness that claims your strength and energy. The surgery that creates unbearable pain. The helplessness and frustrations of being a caregiver. The paycheck that doesn't cover the bills. The wayward child. The abandoned spouse. The grief from the loss of a loved one. The company layoff. Family hurt. Church hurt. And learning to live with a disability. You are probably going through the pruning process right now, or maybe you just came through it.

As we read this passage, verse 3 looks out of place:

You are already clean because of the word which I have spoken to you. (John 15:3)

Why would Jesus tell His disciples they were clean in the midst of a discourse on pruning? The Greek word for pruning can also be translated "cleaning." The Word of God cleanses us, but it also prunes us. The Word of God is sharper than a two-edged sword, and it pierces even to the division of soul and spirit (Hebrews 4:12). Our growth comes through the storms we traverse and from the washing of the Word. Both create fruit.

Abide in Me, and I in you. As the branch cannot bear fruit of itself, unless it abides in the vine, neither can you, unless you abide in Me.

I am the vine, you are the branches. He who abides in Me, and I in him, bears much fruit; for without Me you can do nothing. If anyone does not abide in Me, he is cast out as a branch and is withered; and they gather them and throw them into the fire, and they are burned. (John 15:4-6)

Next, Jesus tells us we can go beyond more fruit and produce "much" fruit. This indicates a progression. When we were children, we started school at a young age. Some of us started in kindergarten, while others attended preschool. No matter where we started, we all began progressing from first grade to second grade and to third grade. Some progressed faster than others, but it continued through high school.

When you entered second grade, you knew more than you did in first grade. When you entered high school, you had much knowledge, and when you graduated, your knowledge base was even greater.

As believers, we can progress if we choose to. Some people are content with getting their toes wet. They settle for a dab of Jesus on Sunday, but they coast through the rest of the week only checking in for a blessing or quick bedtime prayer.

Lord, Thank You for this day. Bless my family. Amen.

But that's not enough for some of us, and it shouldn't be enough for you. So, let's move ahead to bearing much fruit.

John 15:4 and Philippians 4:13 are similar because they both convey the message that it is only through Jesus Christ that we can do anything. I knew the only way I could accomplish the rehabilitation process was through the strength of Christ. I couldn't do it without Him. Are we depending on Christ, or is He our last resort when we can't figure it out? Do we ask Jesus to help us in our smallest endeavors, or do we only take the tough stuff to Him?

You can imagine I have difficulty locating things around the house, especially when they aren't in their place. If I drop something on the floor, Iva helps me find it, but if something has been misplaced, I ask Jesus for help. I can wander around the house searching aimlessly for hours before asking Him to help, or I can go straight to the source. Someone may think that is too trivial to bother the Lord with, but can I remind you that Jesus told us to ask, seek, and knock (Matthew 7:7). The Apostle Paul also commanded us to pray about everything (Philippians 4:6).

Jesus told us that we can do nothing apart from Him. Abiding includes relying on Christ for everything, but abiding goes much deeper than total dependence on the Lord.

The word "abide" means to stay, remain, continue, or dwell. Besides your home, is there a place where you feel comfortable? A place where you can kick off your shoes, go to the fridge, and pour a glass of sweet tea? It isn't your home, but it has all the comforts of home. Your parents' house? Your neighbor? The vacation home or rental you visit annually?

Does Jesus feel at home in your heart? Or does He feel like a visitor? Possibly even a stranger? He cannot feel at home in the heart of sin, nor can He feel relaxed in the heart of someone who has little time for Him.

As teenagers, several of us hung out together all day throughout the summer and on weekends. We moved from one house to another, eating, listening to music, or watching TV. No matter whose house we were visiting, we felt at home, not like visitors.

The reason for that sense of ease was the time we spent together. Do we hang out with Jesus? The *New Application Study Bible* notes that abiding also means we are making the correct choices in life. It goes on to say we must be living in love in obedience to Christ and to others. Are we really abiding?

We have progressed from the pruning process to relying on Christ, and abiding. Here's the verse we all love:

If you abide in Me, and My words abide in you, you will ask what you desire, and it shall be done for you. By this My Father is glorified, that you bear much fruit; so you will be My disciples. (John 15:7-8)

When we abide in Christ, and His words abide in us, we have the promise of answered prayer. Not only must we abide in Christ, but His words, His commandments, and His promises must abide in us.

When I realized blindness was imminent, I didn't know how to pray. Something deep inside didn't make healing a priority. I felt God had bigger plans for me. If He had revealed His plans for writing and ministry at that time, it would have created more fear than losing my sight. I prayed I would never have to live in darkness, and thank God, He answered that prayer.

The prayer I prayed most often was for God to mold me into a vessel He could use. I felt secure as the clay in the mighty hands of the potter. Then I prayed for God to give me the strength and grace necessary to learn everything I needed for the rehabilitation process. Praise Jesus, He answered those prayers.

Sometimes the mountain moves, but sometimes God climbs the mountain with us.

When we genuinely abide, we are so committed to the Lord that we want what He wants. If God's plan for my life did not include healing, I didn't want it. I am not trying to sound like a super Christian, but that is the dedication and devotion someone abiding in Christ possesses. We want what He wants, and not our will. Sounds like the words of Jesus only hours after He gave this message to His disciples.

Friend, you can have that too. You have read the words of Jesus. Abide! He is calling out to you. This isn't some special relationship only accessible to preachers and teachers. It's available to every child of God, but you have to want it.

You have to make time for Jesus. He's not going to force it on you. That's why some Christians feel their prayers never rise above the ceiling.

Do you want a richer relationship with the Lord? I challenge you to wade out a little deeper. Don't settle for getting your feet wet. Dive in wholeheartedly.

Maybe you desire to know God intimately, but there's no way you can add to your already overloaded schedule. That's what the enemy wants you to believe. Whether the enemy is your own flesh or Satan himself, the enemy doesn't want you getting closer to God. The flesh wants to stay in bed a little bit longer. The devil begins to quake when he considers what will happen when you rise early to pray.

The enemy knows things you may not be aware of. He knows how much Jesus loves you and desires communion with you. He knows he loses a foothold when you abide in Christ. He knows your prayers will be answered because you've started praying for the plans of God. He knows you can do all things through Christ who strengthens you. And he knows you have authority over him. That frightens him.

Stop now and pray. Tell Jesus your needs. Confess any sin. He is faithful and just to forgive (1 John 1:9). Seek His cleansing and sanctification. Seek His help in living an obedient life.

Get completely filled with the Holy Spirit. Full to the brim and running over. Soon, you will begin seeing the fruit of the Spirit abounding in your life. You will not merely be existing.

People will notice there's something different about you. That's not a Sunday-only Christian. They will approach you with their prayer requests when they see your faith and belief that prayer changes things.

When we abide in the Vine, we abound in His blessings.

Your life will abound when you abide. Maybe not in money. You won't have less trouble, but you will reap the harvest of blessings. Abiding is the first key to answered prayer. There are two more in upcoming chapters. But take time to get this right before moving ahead.

Lord Jesus, thank You for Your constant love and care. We want to progress. We are done with settling for less. We are going deeper with You. In Jesus' name, Amen.

Stepping Stones

When grace rushes in, frustration rushes out.

Remember what God has done. Ask Him to do it again.

Life can never take us where grace will never find us.

Sometimes Jesus heals, and sometimes He helps.

His glory for His grace. His grace for His glory.

Sometimes the mountain moves, but sometimes God climbs the mountain with us.

When we abide in the Vine, we abound in His blessings.

Scripture

I can do all things through Christ who strengthens me.
(Philippians 4:13)

Abide in Me, and I in you. As the branch cannot bear fruit of itself, unless it abides in the vine, neither can you, unless you abide in Me.

I am the vine, you are *the branches. He who abides in Me, and I in him, bears much fruit; for without Me you can do nothing. If anyone does not abide in Me, he is cast out as a branch and is withered; and they gather them and throw* them *into the fire, and they are burned.* (John 15:4-6)

If you abide in Me, and My words abide in you, you will ask what you desire, and it shall be done for you. By this My Father is glorified, that you bear much fruit; so you will be My disciples. (John 15:7-8)

- https://homeguides.sfgate.com/trimming-grape-vines-produce-bigger-grapes-55810.html

CHAPTER 10

BELIEVE FOR A MIRACLE

Here I am, on the balcony of room 266 watching daylight slip behind the Smoky Mountains. I have fallen in love with Gatlinburg, Tennessee. It is so like God for me to write this particular chapter this week, where it took place. The blue haze drapes over the mountains, in the same way I picture the Holy Spirit descending upon us. God moves mysteriously in these mountains.

This story began at home in Virginia, but it took an incredible side trip to Gatlinburg. In February 2015, we planned our trip to Baltimore for an appointment with my retina specialist. A blanket of snow caused us to postpone. The second appointment was changed when Timmy became sick. Next, a medical conference bumped my appointment into April. Altogether, there were six schedule conflicts for various reasons.

Multiple prayers had bombarded heaven concerning these appointments. Why wouldn't God want me to see the specialist who might be able to halt the progression of my blindness? Even though I hadn't been eligible for the clinical trial, he was on the cutting edge of research. Was God preventing me from returning to Hopkins?

In May, the Baltimore riots broke out. We watched the news in disbelief, as rocks were hurled and stores were burned to the ground.

My appointment was scheduled for the day after Memorial Day. This seventh time, God impressed upon us to cancel, not postpone. Memorial Day weekend 2015 was one of the bloodiest weekends Baltimore had experienced in history.

OK, God, what now? My primary care doctor urged me to see Dr. Donna Maxfield, an ophthalmologist in Roanoke, Virginia. I wondered what the sevens could mean. I paid close attention to the number seven, but it didn't become clear until that special Saturday night in Gatlinburg.

My vision had deteriorated to almost nothing. At times, I prayed blindness would take over, since my vision was aggravating. A hazy glare covered the entire field of vision except for a small line at the bottom. It resembled a window shade pulled down but just short of hitting the window sill.

Trips to the stores left me with headaches from the bright fluorescent lighting. Afterward, I secluded myself in a totally dark room waiting for the headache to subside. I began wearing sunglasses to shop, or I avoided the problem and stayed home.

The steamy July afternoon arrived when I saw Dr. Maxfield. July, the seventh month. In her waiting room, I noticed the glare from the lights. After meeting her, I described the fog I was living in. She examined my eyes, and she revealed the culprit behind my haze.

Cataracts were the cause of these recent changes, not my retinal dystrophy. Dr. Maxfield assured me there was no need to wait for the cataracts to "ripen" in my case, because I needed all the light and vision I could get.

Previously, my doctors had noted the cataracts, but they never went into any detail about them. Dr. Maxfield was different. She explained my vision would not improve much. Surgery would eliminate the haze and headaches.

I could live with that. I was keenly aware God was up to something, especially with the number seven continuing to make appearances. Now with the latest turn of events, I lingered in prayer seeking God's guidance.

I scheduled surgery for October. Summer was busy with my flower gardens, not a great time to take it easy. We already had tickets for one of the biggest southern gospel events in August, the Gatlinburg Gathering. In September, we had our annual beach trip. Things would slow down in October.

Two weeks after my appointment with Dr. Maxfield, I attended the She Speaks conference, a conference for Christian women who write and speak, hosted by Proverbs 31 Ministries. Surrounding the workshops was a refreshing message about faith. God gave me a Scripture to claim.

"Therefore I say to you, whatever things you ask when you pray, believe that you receive them, and you will have them." (Mark 11:24)

Did the Bible say that? Believe God will give you what you request? Jesus said it, but I knew few people who believed it, including myself. I had rarely heard it preached, and I was surrounded by folks who prayed for God's will, as we should. It's like they think God's will excludes miracles.

Praying for God's will and believing we will receive whatever we ask is almost impossible to comprehend. Scripture commands both. Therefore, praying for God's will doesn't rule out believing for a miracle. When we abide in Christ, our desires become His desires, eliminating the possibility of selfish prayer requests. God's will is our ultimate desire, and His will often includes miracles. I learned that vital lesson that summer.

After teaching me the true meaning of faith (complete trust) and giving me this verse, God spoke to me. Not audibly, but a definite message. He specifically conveyed that it wasn't going to be a full restoration of vision, but I would see better after surgery. Much better.

I began asking people to pray, explaining the necessity to genuinely believe God would improve my vision. Silence stared back at me many times. The half-brother of our Lord, James, told us we don't have because we don't ask (James 4:2). Is that why many people don't see miracles? They don't believe, so they don't receive?

Doubt builds walls, but faith knocks walls down.

I boldly told people if they couldn't believe for my miracle, I didn't want them praying for me. Did I really say that? Yes.

Unbelief wasn't going to stop my miracle. We must be careful who we ask to pray for us.

I tried to distance myself from doubt. Believing for a miracle was new territory for me. Every day, the devil asked "what if?" What if my vision doesn't improve? What if I declare God will heal, and He doesn't? What will people think then? My reply, "God will do it. He said He would."

In August, we spent a week in Gatlinburg. Our first stop was Sunday morning worship at Grace Baptist Church. My friend Charlotte always takes me up to the choir loft to sing with the choir. The song was about heaven and blinded eyes being able to see. Charlotte gave me a side hug and exclaimed, "You're going to see one day."

Charlotte knew nothing about my determination to believe for my healing. After church, I shared my story with Charlotte. Imagine my shock when she exclaimed, "I believe it too."

Charlotte reaffirmed her faith in God. He had healed her from cancer. She believed.

The next day, we ran into a friend in Gatlinburg. When I told him my news, he reacted like Charlotte. That conversation rehearsed itself throughout the week. Suddenly, I was no longer encircled by unbelieving Christians.

Countless people prayed for me during the Gatlinburg Gathering. By the end of the week, I was believing for complete healing. I remember God had told me my vision would not be 20/20, but at least my faith had grown enough to ask.

Surround your mountain with people who believe mountains move.

Although I had purchased our seats in February, God intervened. I was seated beside James, who was also legally blind. Not surprising, since the third row is reserved for the visually impaired. As James and I talked, I discovered he had undergone cataract surgery in addition to his other visual problem, just like me. James testified about his improvement in vision after surgery. Only God works like that.

Something was special about Saturday night. God's presence was so real you could reach out and touch Him. Dr. Jon Bowman took us on a jet tour through the Bible looking at all the times the number seven appears. In Scripture, seven means *complete* or *perfect*. Seven is also the number for God, but six is the number for man. I clung to every word of the sermon, but there was no a-ha moment that connected the message to my situation.

I think the number seven was meant to draw my attention to what happened next. Between songs, several people had shared their testimonies about healing. The man on stage testified that he was cancer free as he praised the Lord. This one touched me more than the others, because we had been praying for him. I looked down, trying to wipe all the tears away. When I looked toward the stage, Karen Peck began singing.

The piano lifted its voice. Guitars hummed harmoniously, and drums vibrated the floor. Voices sang in worship to God as I remained silent.

My vision had changed. The haze covering my eyes had lifted. Another large video screen had become visible. It wasn't 20/20 vision, but I'm not sure what 20/20 would look like.

Then it disappeared. Clouds covered my eyes once again. The video screen on my left side dropped out of sight where it had hidden from me all week. Vision was back to a dim normal. Normal for me, that is.

What caused temporary clarity? The tears? It had to be the tears. I kept this treasure to myself. I asked God to reveal what happened, and I waited.

As my surgery drew near, it became increasingly difficult to believe for healing. Arrows of disbelief continually struck me. The devil berated me, and few people encouraged me. How I wished I could return to Gatlinburg.

Discouragement caught up with me. One afternoon, my emotions cut loose, and a flood of tears fell. Suddenly, it dawned on me. My vision did not clear up after crying, like it did in Gatlinburg. If tears did not enable me to see temporarily, what did? Had God shown me what the world would look like post-surgery?

I was making the bed one morning as my cat stretched out grabbing blankets. She liked playing that game. I was listening to a sermon podcast by Dr. Tony Evans. When I heard his words, I knew God had answered my question about those few minutes of clear vision. A hallelujah shout sent my kitty scrambling, in search of a quieter place.

Elijah had heard rain before it began raining (1 Kings 18:41). He reported to King Ahab that a downpour was nearby, but God allowed Elijah to hear the inaudible. Then Elijah prayed seven times. Yes, seven! Afterward, the rain began.

It made perfect sense. God allowed me to see what in reality I could not see. Not a vision, but a change in vision. A preview of what was to come.

Before then, I never would have accredited something so peculiar to God. Not only had God gave me a preview of what I could soon see, but He opened my eyes to His supernatural ways. Never again will I discount someone's testimony because it sounds preposterous.

God makes the impossible possible.

In the wee hours of dawn, I took inventory of our home, what everything looked like. I knew when I came home from the first surgery it would change. Dr. Maxfield prayed with me before they wheeled me back.

I went to bed when I got home to sleep off the anesthesia. Timmy was outside when I awoke. I walked into my bathroom wearing a patch covering the left eye. Even with the patch, I spotted lighthouses on my shower curtain. I squealed in excitement. That morning, they had been blobs.

I slowly walked down our hallway. Pictures lined the walls. I had forgotten them. As I entered our living room, I quickly found the flowers on the drapes. I had forgotten them too. Tears of joy began to run down my cheeks as I thanked God for His miracle.

Perhaps the most beautiful sight my eyes beheld was the cross at church. Memories of it had faded along with my vision. I walked toward the cross without anyone's help. I testified about the miracle God had accomplished. After church, a man said, "God really does miracles."

Another one said, "I think that's what I need to do. Believe God will answer."

In the following weeks, I admired a full moon in all its brightness. I couldn't remember the moon being so large. From the doorway, my eyes captured the bright-yellow mums lining the patio. I marveled as raindrops fell from heaven. I still am in awe of them.

I glorified God when I could see the fall colors. Traffic lights and signs along the highway now came into view. Winter arrived with the promise of snow. I erupted with the glee of a little child waiting for the snowflakes to fall. I had longed to see snowflakes dance toward the ground.

Are you in need of a miracle today? Are you in need of God's healing? Perhaps someone you love needs that miracle. Let me tell you something, friend. God heals. I could continue writing about the times He has healed me. I have been healed from emotional pain as well as physical pain.

God heals marriages. He heals churches. He heals brokenness. He heals our bodies, and most importantly, He heals our souls.

How can we possess the faith that believes beyond a shadow of a doubt that God will heal? The faith that believes God will miraculously provide? The faith that believes God supernaturally protects?

Miracles never ceased. People ceased believing.

We lack the knowledge and wisdom to know which prayers are according to God's will. Sometimes Scripture helps us, but many times, the answer is not between the covers of our Bible. Therefore, we must believe for a "Yes." No one can understand the mind of God. Believe for your miracle while praying for His will. That is biblical. It's not one way or another.

First, we must believe. We need to cleanse ourselves of all doubt. Remove every speck of it.

I feared the plans God had for Timmy when he had leukemia. As I have matured as a Christian, I learned to trust God. And I learned to pray expecting my answer.

Friend, I have struggled with trusting God to do the impossible. Will God do for you what He didn't do for another? Satan doesn't want us to believe. People don't want to believe. They fear it will not happen. I would rather say I trusted God to heal, but it was not His plan, rather than lack the confidence in Him to do the impossible.

Admitting we have a problem is always half the battle. A father desperately wanted a miracle for his son. He knew he needed to trust Jesus for his boy's healing. He also knew his faith had some holes in it.

The father brought his demon-possessed son to Jesus' disciples, but they got nowhere with the boy. Frustrated, the man approached Jesus, explaining his son's behavior. The spirit threw the boy into the fire. He caused him to roll frantically on the ground, gnashing his teeth and foaming at the mouth like a rabid animal. Can you feel this father's panic as he told Jesus the disciples couldn't help his son?

Jesus had been healing people and casting out demons. Jesus empowered His disciples to do miracles too. What about this father and son? Why were they different? Disappointment cut the father like a sharp knife. Jesus did it for others. Why not him? Why not his boy?

We can empathize with this desperate father. All the treatments have failed, and the new one that was going to be your miracle didn't work either. Hopelessness has hit an all-time low.

He answered him and said, "O faithless generation, how long shall I be with you? How long shall I bear with you? Bring him to Me." Then they brought him to Him. And when he saw Him, immediately the spirit convulsed him, and he fell on the ground and wallowed, foaming at the mouth. (Mark 9:19-20)

Then Jesus asked the father how long his son had been in this condition. The father explained that it began during childhood. The spirit often threw him into the fire or water, possibly in an attempt to take this boy's life.

"But if You can do anything, have compassion on us and help us."

Jesus said to him, "If you can believe, all things are *possible to him who believes."*

Immediately the father of the child cried out and said with tears, "Lord, I believe; help my unbelief!" (Mark 9:22b-24)

Did this man really say, "If You can do anything...?" Was he so distraught he forgot whom he was speaking to? Jesus can do anything He desires, but that is exactly what you and I say when we don't believe. We might not be as blunt as this father, but he was being honest. God knows our hearts. Are we being truthful with ourselves when it comes to how much we believe God will do for us?

He believed, but he struggled to wholeheartedly believe. He knew his uncertainty could interfere with the miracle. Hence the request from this desperate father, "Lord, I believe. Help my unbelief."

This man had residual doubt. His son had suffered under the control of a demonic spirit far too long. We can understand his plight. We have prayed for decades for That loved one who needs salvation. The special needs child you have been praying for. The addict that never gets deliverance. The cancer prognosis that gets worse, in spite of your prayers.

This father was at the end of his rope. He had already tied the knot and was holding on. What a blow to his faith when the men closest to Jesus couldn't free his son from his tormenter. Now, he cried out, "Help my unbelief!"

Friend, is that what we are crying out? Lord, help my unbelief. I want to believe, really, Lord, I do, but unbelief chases me down.

Believing isn't going to come easily, because the enemy of our souls doesn't want us to possess that assurance. He wants Christians to doubt God. He planted doubt in the mind of Eve when he tempted her in the perfect Garden of Eden. He wants us to live in unbelief. He loves these folks who claim miracles ceased. If miracles ceased, how did God save them? That's the greatest miracle of all. To see a heart black with sin cleansed and changed.

Thank God for the shield of faith. We can take that shield and cover ourselves. The shield of a Roman soldier measured about four feet long and over two feet wide. It was large enough for the soldier to crouch behind and avoid the arrows of the enemy. And that is what we possess, a shield of faith. We take up that shield and stop the fiery darts of the devil. That is how we protect our faith. That is how we help our unbelief.

In the words of Jesus Christ Himself, "all things *are* possible to him who believes." (Mark 9:23b) What do we do when our faith wanes in the face of discouragement? We pray like the father of this tormented boy. We ask the Lord to help our unbelief. Jesus faithfully grants us what we need. If our desire is to trust Him completely, He will deliver.

Jesus cast the demon from the boy, and the evil spirit departed kicking and screaming, leaving the boy limp on the ground. But he was alive, and he was free of the enemy. Can you imagine the joy of his father? Can you hear the worship and praise to the Lord? Because he believed. Friend, that is exactly what we must do. Believe and ask God to help any unbelief. Nothing backs up a prayer like faith in God to do the impossible.

Then the disciples asked why they were unable to rescue the boy from the spirit. Jesus explained that sometimes it requires praying and fasting. Jesus could have been referring to the type of fallen angel that had possessed the boy. Demons, like holy angels, have different hierarchies.

But He could have been telling them to push. I have a T-shirt that says, "Strong Women PUSH." PUSH! Pray until something happens. Along with our faith in God, we must PUSH. That can become as wearisome as fighting darts of doubt, but it is woven throughout Scripture.

In Luke chapter 18, Jesus told the parable of the persistent widow (Luke 18:1-8). His point being that men should always pray without losing heart. If this widow could push until a greedy judge who didn't love God could give her what she wanted, what more will God do? God, who loves us. God, our heavenly Father. God, who has given us many precious promises.

Then in Matthew, Jesus commands us to ask, seek, and knock. The author of Hebrews urges us to approach the throne of grace with boldness (Hebrews 4:16).

Periodically, I am afflicted with back pain due to arthritis and scoliosis. The day prior to speaking at a women's conference, it flared up in an extreme way. I tried hot showers, rest, creams, and medicine, but nothing soothed the gnawing agony taunting me. I prayed. I believed. I resisted the devil. I prayed more. I grew weary in praying. I grew weary in persisting.

Despite my misery, I went to my church to set up my table and pray over the seats. When I walked in, my burden was evident, along with the strong scent of menthol cream. Sister Nikki immediately recognized my pain.

Pastor Ray and his family laid hands on me, anointed me, and prayed. I was wearing another T-shirt that day. One that read, "Somebody's praying, somebody's believing, somebody's receiving." This wasn't the first time I have experienced healing from pain in my church. We believe. Before I left church that evening, my pain had almost dissipated. The next morning, I felt great.

Do we give up too early? Do we fail to prevail in prayer because we get bogged down in the pushing? We tire of knocking.

Why is praying so difficult? Because we are fighting a battle down on our knees. We are engaging in spiritual warfare in heavenly places.

Ah, but we have good news. We don't have to battle alone, nor in our own strength.

When our strength evades us, God's strength will invade us.

Finally, my brethren, be strong in the Lord and in the power of His might. (Ephesians 6:10)

Like the father who despised his unbelief, we turn to the Lord. When we tire of praying with no answers, we can wait on the Lord and be strengthened with the power of His might. This is a wonderful promise to memorize and claim when our faith begins to wane. It is God who empowers us to believe and to push.

Friend, you are a mighty prayer warrior in the army of God. You have drawn nigh to Christ as you abide in the vine. His desires have become your desires. Now, you trust Him to deliver. You trust God to be faithful to His promises. You trust Him to heal. You trust Him for your breakthrough. And you are praying without ceasing. Praying until something happens. You know how to utilize your shield of faith, and stop the enemy's fiery darts.

I am proud of you! I know what a bondage unbelief can be. You know the promises. Now, get on your knees and PUSH!

Pray, believe, persist, receive.

Heavenly Father, You give us Your strength, power, and might to believe and remain constant in prayer. We need that, Lord, because doubt peeks around every corner. Thank You for the miracles we are going to see. I believe an abundance of miracles awaits us, because I know what happens when we believe and pray. In Jesus' name, all glory to You, Amen.

Stepping Stones

Doubt builds walls, but faith knocks walls down.

Surround your mountain with people who believe mountains move.

God makes the impossible possible.

Miracles never ceased. People ceased believing.

When our strength evades us, God's strength will invade us.

Pray, believe, persist, receive.

Scripture

"Therefore I say to you, whatever things you ask when you pray, believe that you receive them, and you will have them." (Mark 11:24)

"But if You can do anything, have compassion on us and help us."

Jesus said to him, "If you can believe, all things are possible to him who believes."

Immediately the father of the child cried out and said with tears, "Lord, I believe; help my unbelief!" (Mark 9:22b-24)

Finally, my brethren, be strong in the Lord and in the power of His might. (Ephesians 6:10)

CHAPTER 11

EXERCISING OUR FAITH

Gail answered her phone, but when I opened my mouth to speak, the only sound I could make were gasps accompanying my tears. Between sobs, I found the words.

"I got lost! When I was walking, I didn't know where I was!"

"Carolyn! Are you at home now? What happened?"

I took a deep breath, so Gail could make sense of my words.

"I went for a walk, and I had to get around two parked cars, because we don't have sidewalks up here. When I thought I was past them, I couldn't find the curb with my cane again. I panicked, and I didn't know if I was in the middle of the street or if I had drifted into a driveway. The whole time my cane searched for the curb, I was praying, asking God for help."

I could still taste the fear choking me as each step resulted in another failed attempt to find something besides asphalt. My mind raced, but refused to think straight, or I would have faced the sun. Even with dark sunglasses, it shone brightly as it kissed the winter horizon.

I continued, "Finally, my cane found the curb. So, I thanked God thinking I was on my way home, but when I reached the corner, it wasn't my street."

More sobs and another deep breath.

"Gail, the curb is my mental map. My curb meets grass. This curb met more curbing."

"Oh, my word, Carolyn!"

I explained, "I asked Siri (Apple's personal assistant on the smartphone) for my location. Then I lifted my sunglasses revealing a pine tree towering above me, and I knew where I was. Siri confirmed it with an address. I'd been in the middle of the street, but I ended up on the opposite side heading in the wrong direction."

Gail sensed the danger I could have been in. I could have been hit by a car. I could still be wondering around aimlessly. Even worse than the could-have-beens, was the self-confidence I lost.

I went on to clue Gail in on the fact that nothing exists to help blind people with navigating. The few apps and devices that exist were not suitable for my needs. Most of them lacked accuracy.

"Why did God allow this?" I was referring to the new vision God had blessed me with after the cataract surgery. He could have left my vision like it was. Yes, He got me safely home, but nothing like this had ever happened before the surgery. Now, I could sit and stare at beauties I couldn't see before, but my closest vision was unreliable.

Gail's voice sounded reassuring, "God wouldn't bring you this far for no reason. He has to have a purpose in it all."

But we couldn't figure out what His purpose was. Gail desperately wanted to help, but she had no idea she was steering me in the direction God wanted me to go. "What about a guide dog?" Gail suggested with a gleam of hope in her voice.

"No, I don't walk enough. I don't work outside the house. Plus, I would have to go live with the dog and train for six months. There is no way I can be gone that long."

When I lost the majority of my sight three years earlier, I contacted a guide dog school. At that point, I lacked the necessary cane skills for safe navigation. The school heavily advised against a dog. They convinced me a cane would never let me down, but a dog would. My mobility instructor from the DBVI wasn't pro-dog either. It appeared as if the white cane were my only hope. And now, it had proved undependable.

Gail's words kept ringing in my ears after we ended our conversation. I entertained the idea of a guide dog. It seemed like a dog could lead me around parked cars, but I was uncertain about the information I had received. Soon, I would learn it was all myths.

Walking was the only independent activity I enjoyed except for the technological world. Wherever I went, I went with Timmy, hanging on to his elbow, otherwise known as sighted-guide.

Walking confidently and safely through my neighborhood streets was a process. I began with one block, and I slowly increased my route until I was walking one mile daily. The white cane is basically an extension of your hand. I felt the entire path through the cane. I knew the exact location of curbing and grass. I memorized the dips and curves. I had a mental map, and I dared not veer from my route.

Walking the streets gets complicated with parked cars. I was careful to prevent my cane from touching a car. If it did, it would do no damage, since the cane would run under the car, but people behave funny about things like that, so I kept an imaginary buffer around all vehicles.

I became comfortable with speed walking, and I thought I could travel this route even if I were totally blind. Now, I was afraid to ever step out of my house again. My favorite hobby, walking, had been ripped away from me. Months of work disappeared in a moment.

The next day, I called the only person I knew who ever had a guide dog. She reminded me she had worked from home also. She even recommended a school, Guiding Eyes for the Blind, in New York. Training was only for three weeks, not six months. That is when I seriously began inquiring about the school and what life with a guide dog would be like.

I prayed about it, and I stepped out of my comfort zone into my faith zone to go to New York and train with this black beauty that is now by my side.

My exercise routine changed. In addition to physical exercise, I had to exercise my faith muscles. Getting the nerve to walk again required faith.

Exercise your faith for a healthy heart.

My mobility instructor came out to work with me as a refresher course. I needed to get in shape to attend guide dog school. I began rebuilding my confidence, exercising my body, and exercising my faith simultaneously.

Attending the school required me to fly to New York's LaGuardia airport alone. The thought of the Big Apple frightened this small-town girl. I refused to think about it. Just trust God. That's what I kept telling myself as those thoughts taunted me every day.

A week before my flight, more alarming hurdles stood in my path. No direct flight was available. My anxiety level rose. Two days prior to my departure, a bomb exploded in New York City. Another terrorist. More faith was needed to jump these hurdles that made my heart beat faster.

Friend, you have felt fear's grip. Maybe, you struggle with it right now. Perhaps you are facing a surgery, and anxiety looms over you concerning the results. Maybe you are preparing to attend a new school, start a new job, or move to another city, and you feel a bit apprehensive. Perhaps you are caring for sick or aging parents, and you feel drained. You have to make decisions and lifestyle changes. Possibly, you are raising your grandchildren. You don't know how you can continue with all the demands on your schedule. Or the demands on your paycheck. Has God asked you to move into a new calling, but you can't bring yourself to take the first step?

Maybe, like me, God has disappointed you. That's OK. God knows when we are displeased with Him, so we should admit it. It doesn't mean He is wrong. God has never been wrong, and He never will be. It proves His ways are vastly different than our ways.

I can say that because on that day, the day I was lost, I was disappointed in God. I was angry with Him, but I didn't camp out there. That is the important part. Admit it, but move on from there.

I failed to grasp God's purpose, or what He was doing. I struggled with that. I have learned it's OK for God to keep me in the dark, no pun intended.

I don't need to know like I think I need to know.

I should have trusted God. I should have acted in faith rather than allowing my flesh to get carried away. We all need to exercise faith, and the result will be healthy hearts. Just like physical exercise strengthens your physical heart, faith-strengthening exercises make our minds, our souls, and our hearts, where our emotions are seated, a healthier place. Let's look at Psalm 37:3-5:

Trust in the Lord, and do good;
Dwell in the land, and feed on His faithfulness.
Delight yourself also in the Lord,
And He shall give you the desires of your heart.

Commit your way to the Lord,
Trust also in Him,
And He shall bring it *to pass.*

Notice verse three begins with "Trust in the Lord" and verse five also commands us to trust. I call this passage a trust sandwich. I was probably craving white bread on the day I came up with that. Let's see what is necessary to make this sandwich.

Think of your favorite sandwich. Maybe it's a BLT, turkey and swiss, or ham and cheese. So, we have two slices of bread or perhaps a wrap. That's our trust here. Then we add other ingredients: meat, cheese, lettuce, tomatoes, and our favorite condiment.

That's what we are doing in this passage. Just like each ingredient on your sandwich has health benefits, all the ingredients for deeper faith are sandwiched between these verses.

Each verse starts with a commandment followed by a promise. The psalmist David declared, "Trust in the Lord." Not in ourselves. Not in the doctor. Not in the counselor. Not even in the pastor. Trust in the Lord. When we possess firm faith in God, our reluctance to move forward will dissipate.

For example, I became excited about my New York adventure. During the last week of training, the school takes a day trip to Manhattan with the dogs. That was as scary as flying to New York, but I started looking forward to it rather than dreading it.

God creates calm. Unbelief creates chaos.

The next command is "Do good." Obedience. Purity. Right living. If we resolve to put feet on our faith, but we continue to entertain sin, God isn't obliged to fulfill His promises attached to these commands.

Matthew Henry calls this "Confide and conform." I like that, but I prefer "transform and trust." Holiness must grow out of a transformed life, not a strict regimen of laws to follow. It reminds me of the old hymn, "Trust and obey, for there's no other way."

Our first promise is the benefit of transforming and trusting: "dwell in the land." What kind of promise is this? In the Old Testament, it referred to dwelling in the Promised Land. Today, while we might not live in the Promised Land, we do dwell upon the promises of God. He has given us precious promises throughout Scripture. Promises for grace, promises for strength, and promises for peace.

We are also dwelling with God. As we walk in faith, we hold His hand. He is right beside us the entire way. Through the pain. Through the dilemma, and yes, even through a trip to New York.

So far, our trust sandwich has two ingredients, trusting and doing good. The benefit is God's promises, but we have one more benefit in this verse. "Feed on His faithfulness." Isn't God faithful to deliver on His promises? Pause right now and give Him some praise for His faithfulness.

Jesus Christ, our Shepherd, is faithful to feed us. He provides for us. We lack nothing. Knowing that He supplies all we need makes trusting Him easy.

Our third command appears in verse four: "Delight in the Lord." What does "delight in the Lord" mean? Delight simply means to please. We please God, or do we? Is the Lord pleased with our character? What about our homes? Does the Lord look in on us at the dinner table and smile? Does our life delight God?

Does Jesus feel at home at your home?

Delighting in the Lord also means we are pleased with Him. In everything we are pleased, as opposed to grumbling, angry, or disappointed. A deep-rooted confidence in God enables us to endure life's struggles without complaining. So, we see why delighting in the Lord fits nicely in our trust sandwich.

Here is the promise we all love. God will give us the desires of our heart. I hate to burst your bubble, but this does not mean God gives us a blank check. We want it to mean that. God doesn't grant us every desire our flesh craves, like that new car, or that new job. He may not give us a new bank account or the perfectly behaved child. What God will give us is greater than anything we can think or ask. God places His desires in our hearts.

We desire what God desires.

What if God's desire is for us to quit our jobs, sell everything we own, and live in a mud hut in Africa as a missionary? That may be God's desire for someone, but if that is God's will for your life, you will love that mud hut in Africa when you see souls coming to Jesus.

God doesn't cram His desires down our throats. We can obediently submit to the Lord, or we can elect to be displeasing to Him. In my life, God's plans have been better than anything I could have imagined. Sweet friend, He will do the same for you.

Verse five commands us to commit our way to the Lord. That is guidance. Trust and guidance are similar because we trust God to direct our steps.

The Lord has a way in which He wants us to walk. Our job is to walk in it.

Seeking God's direction connects back to those desires in the previous verse. He equips us in whatever He calls us to do. Whether it's a missions project in Africa, teaching a children's Sunday school class, speaking, or traveling to New York and training with a guide dog, God will never give us any desire without giving us the ability and wisdom to bring it to fruition.

Let's look at how this works. Training with a dog is quite demanding and exhausting. God gave me the wisdom to inquire about the amount of walking necessary at school. Months before going to school, I began getting in shape. God enabled me to get up early each morning and reach that goal. Once I began training with Iva in New York, I felt pretty good when everyone else started tiring out.

We worked long days beginning at 5:30 AM, and sometimes not ending until 9:30 PM. Our schedule included obedience at 6:00 AM, breakfast, load up for the White Plains training facility by 8:00 AM, morning routes, lunch, afternoon routes, return to the school for lectures, and dinner. Evenings were filled with grooming, playtime with our dogs, and extra work on trouble areas. Training was mentally exhausting too. Our brains were overloaded with learning commands and all the do's and don'ts of guide dog work.

Yes, I was exhausted, but since I had disciplined myself for months prior to class, I was the last one standing at the end of the first week. This is why we commit our way to the Lord.

So, we have trust, obedience, delighting in the Lord, and committing to His ways. Those are all the ingredients for this trust sandwich. We add one more slice of trust, and look at our final promise. The words we long to hear: He will bring this to pass. Isn't that a wonderful promise? This will pass.

The dilemma you find yourself in today. It will pass. Your health crisis will pass. That financial crunch will pass. Sometimes knowing it will pass is the only comfort we have in some of our ordeals.

When we bite into these passages, this trust sandwich, we are blessed. We feed on His faithfulness. We are granted the desires of our hearts, and we know our trials will pass.

Wouldn't you agree that our trust levels change? Sometimes, I feel so secure in trusting God, but the day I couldn't find the curb, I felt like part of the "O ye of little faith" group. Do you ever feel like that? You've been there. You know that feeling. You trust God until...that something that makes you tremble arises. That faith muscle needs some exercise.

Iva and I walk almost daily. We include some hills, but when we take on a steep incline, my muscles scream. My body begins perspiring. My breathing gets harder. Iva's pace slows as she starts panting. Steep hills are not in my exercise routine. It shocks my body when we tackle them.

Life is similar. Your world is peaceful and filled with joy. Your prayer life is rich. You are singing praise songs until...the phone call, the knock on the door, or the doctor visit.

That is when we need to stretch our faith muscles. Let's compare this to physical exercise, which can be as beneficial to the heart as medication, according to Johns Hopkins expert Kerry Stewart. "Exercise works like beta-blocker medication to slow the heart rate and lower blood pressure (at rest and also when exercising). Johns Hopkins research has shown that when combined with strength training, regular aerobic exercise such as cycling, brisk walking, or swimming can reduce the risk of developing diabetes by over 50 percent."*

If physical exercise can produce such major advantages to our heart, imagine what wonders we will see when we begin exercising our faith. How do we exercise our faith? Dr. Tony Evans says that faith is acting like God is telling the truth. Faith is an action. I used to think faith was what we believe in our minds, but it makes sense that faith is active. Pastor Ray says, "Put some feet on your faith."

Faith is not just a mind-set. We are not referring to the Christian faith when we are using the word "faith" here. We are talking about the "For All I Trust Him" faith. For All I Trust Him. That kind of faith is an action. It moves, like when we exercise. It involves action. Our faith muscles are not going to be strong unless we use them. They will continue to be anemic as long as we sit on the proverbial couch.

Faith is demonstrated by our movement, not by our mouth.

Noah put his faith into action by building the ark. Daniel and his three Hebrew friends acted in faith by refusing to conform to the world. Moses acted in faith when the Red Sea parted. He didn't stand there with the Egyptians on their heels and say, "God, I trust You, so we will stand here and wait." Moses exercised faith when he lifted his rod. Faith is an action.

Faith is something you do, not just something you believe. We can say we trust God, but we need to demonstrate our faith, like Noah, Daniel, and Moses. We need to show God we trust Him.

I returned to the streets of my neighborhood and started walking short distances. This gives literal meaning to walking by faith, not by sight, especially when you can't see what is in front of you. Each step was a step of faith, a physical step and a spiritual step.

Faith is walking, not just talking.

I put my faith to work. It showed no faith to sit in the house and tell God I trusted Him. That isn't faith. That is unbelief. I had to demonstrate my faith. Because if I really believed God's Word, I would be back out there walking again. Soon, my route totaled three miles daily.

Next, I had to exercise my faith with flying to New York. When we learned about the layover, my husband offered to do several things. He could drive me there. He offered to fly with me and then fly home. I could have also taken the train, but I exercised faith. We trusted God and He was faithful when He provided someone to meet me during my layover.

When my husband woke me in the middle of the night with the news about the explosion, my response was, "You know this is Satan, and we have to trust God."

Honestly, it was a major step out of my comfort zone just to attend a school away from home for three weeks. If you knew me well, you would know how far from normal that was for me.

When we exercise our faith, God gives us healthy hearts. Not a physically healthy heart like you get from walking, but a healthy emotional heart. What God did for me, He will do for you too.

I wasn't praying for a guide dog. I was praying for healing. Complete healing, but something needed healing more than my eyes. My broken heart. Iva was the glue God used to mend the pieces of my heart back together. Iva is more than a guide. The relationship between guide and handler is unique. We have an extremely deep bond. She is my best friend, my helper, and my baby.

During this guide dog journey, my faith experienced a growth spurt. My faith muscles were strengthened, but the blessings continue to flow in. These were the desires God gave me, not the ones I chose.

Iva gave me a confidence I have not experienced since losing the majority of my sight. I can walk faster and safer with my new eyes. We even run short distances. Who would have thought I would love running? I am not athletic by any stretch of the imagination.

When I returned home, doors of independence continued to swing open. I began taking the bus downtown, just Iva and I. We went to places I hadn't been in over twenty years by myself. We spent ten days alone in Gatlinburg on our last writing retreat.

What I did not expect was joy. Iva has brought joy into my life. She showers me with kisses. She does so many silly things that a day never passes without laughter.

The day I got lost seemed like one of the worst days in my life, but it became one of the best. A guide dog wasn't even on my radar prior to that. God planted His desire in my heart, a desire that healed my heart. I am perfectly content with vision loss, especially with a guide dog. I no longer seek healing. I realize some people cannot grasp that, but I need a whole heart more than I need vision. The joy Iva has brought into our home is incredible.

I would have missed out on all these blessings, the independence and joy, if I hadn't acted in faith. If I had not trusted God with the airlines and everything that seemed foreign to me. These are the desires God gives us. God knows what He is doing, better than we can think or ask. His desires are extraordinary, but we have to walk in faith. I never could have dreamed of this abundant life, but God purposed it and set it into motion.

What blessings have we missed by not walking in faith? Why should we continue letting them pass us by? The Word of God says the just live by faith (Hebrews 10:38). Are we living by faith? Friend, we are overcomers, and we have victory through our faith (1 John 5:4).

Are you ready to step out of your comfort zone? What is God asking you to do in order to prove your faith? He has something terrific planned for you, but you must take the first step.

This week, I challenge you to pray and examine your life. Ask God what He wants you to do. Start with one thing. You don't need to make a list. Ask God what that one step of faith looks like in your life.

Step out of your comfort zone into your faith zone.

You can do it! I can say that with confidence because I know God, and He will enable you to do everything He calls you to do.

If each of us does this, can you imagine the testimonies we would have? Testimonies about trusting God. Testimonies of answered prayers. If we began exercising faith, can you imagine the desires God will grant us? We cannot even imagine because it is so awesome. What about the encouragement we can offer others, because of what the Lord has done for us?

I don't know what God has planned for you, but I know He has a plan because I have seen what God has done in my life. Don't trust me. Trust God.

Lord, grant us the courage to step out in faith. Help us trust You more. Thank You for giving us the desires of our hearts when we commit our way to You. Thank You for all You have done and all the mighty things You will do. In Jesus' name, Amen.

Stepping Stones

Exercise our faith for healthy hearts.

I don't need to know like I think I need to know.

God creates calm. Unbelief creates chaos.

We desire what God desires.

Faith is demonstrated by our movement, not by our mouth.

Faith is walking, not just talking.

Step out of your comfort zone into your faith zone.

Scripture

Trust in the Lord, and do good;
Dwell in the land, and feed on His faithfulness.
Delight yourself also in the Lord,
And He shall give you the desires of your heart.

Commit your way to the Lord,
Trust also in Him,
And He shall bring it *to pass.* (Psalm 37:3-5)

- https://www.hopkinsmedicine.org/health/healthy_heart /move_more/seven-heart-benefits-of-exercise

CHAPTER 12

TEN ANCHORS FOR ANY STORM

The first time we vacationed in the Outer Banks of North Carolina, we didn't receive a warm welcome. The people were great. They always are, but the Atlantic roared with anger. The winds howled, pelting sand at us whenever we tried to walk on the beach. We barely had one fair weather day before a nor'easter made an unexpected appearance.

We tried to fill those stormy days with shopping since it rained horizontally. Then we learned the low-lying roads flooded easily, so we resorted to our ocean-front room. Each morning, we bundled up and explored the beach, amazed at the evidence the high tide had left behind. The shoreline changed daily.

Thankfully, we avoided the flooding and dodged the tornadoes. We salvaged two sunny days before going home.

Storms in life often drag on for what seems like eternity, sometimes leaving the landscape of our lives vastly different. In Acts chapter 27, the Apostle Paul takes us on a stormy journey with him. This was no pleasure cruise. Paul wasn't catching some rays and much-needed rest and relaxation. Paul was a prisoner. That's bad enough, but the storms they encountered on their voyage were horrific. First, they set sail during the most dangerous time to begin a journey. Gentle breezes turned into Euroclydon, much like a hurricane. Sometimes, life is calm right before the strongest storms, catching us off guard.

The massive ship was no match for the battering winds and waves that drove it into the Syrtis Sands, otherwise known as the Graveyard of Ships because of its numerous shipwrecks. The passengers tossed everything except essentials overboard in a desperate attempt to lighten the ship. In hopeless times, we become desperate.

Days without sun and nights without stars passed. Unable to see ahead, they feared crashing into rocks. When hope evades us, we see nothing but disaster. That is when we must trust God to steer our ships.

God sent an angel to encourage Paul, telling him they would all survive. Imagine that! The great Apostle Paul needed encouragement. Paul needed a reminder to fear not. Certainly, if the author of most of the New Testament felt some angsts, we will too. In the midst of our storms, we have God's promises. They are His gentle reminders to calm us.

In this final chapter, we will examine ten promises to help us weather our storms. I prayerfully selected the hidden jewels we don't normally keep on the tip of our tongues. Promises we may be less familiar with.

Promise 1

This hope *we have as an anchor of the soul, both sure and steadfast, and which enters the* Presence *behind the veil, where the forerunner has entered for us,* even *Jesus, having become High Priest forever according to the order of Melchizedek. (*Hebrews 6:19-20)

We begin with our anchor, Jesus Christ. We may not perceive the anchor as a symbol of hope, like the ancient world. The writer of Hebrews obviously was familiar with this symbolism.

When is an anchor used? Not on the days when we can kick back and relax soaking in the sun. The anchor is lowered when the waves get choppy, the breeze picks up, and the sun fades from sight.

Once the anchor rests on the ocean floor, it is out of sight. Invisible. We cannot watch the anchor work, but we see the effects of its work. Friend, that is how Jesus works in our lives, behind the scenes. Unseen.

Notice that an anchor doesn't remove us from the storm. Our ship still braves the tempest. The winds and waves are still intense.

The anchor doesn't stop the storm. It stabilizes the ship until the storm passes by.

We sense the anchor is at work when our ship stays steady. We aren't tossed around violently crashing into other ships. We endure the storm, but we escape shipwreck. On its own, this promise offers us encouragement, but God doesn't stop there. He gives us evidence.

We trust Jesus Christ, our anchor because of who He is. Not only our anchor, but He is the forerunner and our High Priest (v. 20). To further understand this, let's peek at the Old Testament and the covenant, before Jesus came on the scene.

Each year, the high priest went into the Holy of Holies to offer sacrifices on behalf of the people. This was the Day of Atonement, but it had to be repeated annually to redeem the people from their sins. The people couldn't enter that holy place, only the high priest.

Christ changed everything with the New Covenant, when Jesus became our sacrifice, once and for all (Hebrews 7:27). After His death, resurrection, and ascension, He stepped into the heavenly Holy of Holies where He advocates on our behalf as our High Priest.

The promise of a steadfast anchor becomes even more precious because our anchor is Jesus. The one who died for us and now intercedes as our High Priest.

Promise 2

The Lord will fight for you, and you shall hold your peace." (Exodus 14:14)

The bills mounting up in your mailbox. Not your battle, but the Lord's. That rebellious child. Not your battle, but the Lord's. That illness. Not your battle, but the Lord's. That problem with your co-worker or boss. Not your battle, but the Lord's.

We must be good stewards of our resources. We can't let our bills pile up while we go on a Hawaiian vacation and expect God to bless careless spending. But when we have done everything within our means to keep up and not overspend, when a medical emergency results in a financial avalanche, God will make a way.

God is for us, not against us.

We don't have to create battle strategies when God says, "Here, let Me handle that."

Moses spoke this promise to the children of Israel as they stood at the edge of the Red Sea with the Egyptians on their heels. Things appeared about as hopeless as it gets. Surrounded by armies and water, they were trapped. Have you ever felt like that? Like no escape route exists? In the prior verse, Moses told them to stop being afraid. We've discussed fear at length in this book, and this promise gives us reason not to fear. The Lord fights for us. When we pray, we are essentially saying, "Lord, here is my predicament. Help!"

We persist in prayer. We believe God is at work, because God says the battle belongs to Him.

Notice the last four words of this promise. It's actually a command to hush. Silence! Those wandering Israelites were famous for their murmuring and complaining. They became enraged with Moses and Aaron. They even became angry with God. Certainly, God tired of their moaning and groaning, but He parted the Red Sea, making a way for them.

When we pray and claim this promise, let's remember to hush. Let God fight the battle. The only words from our lips should be praise and gratitude.

Promise 3

When you pass through the waters, I will be with you;
And through the rivers, they shall not overflow you.
When you walk through the fire, you shall not be burned,
Nor shall the flame scorch you. (Isaiah 43:2)

I live in a flood-prone area. Locals respect the power of water with the memory of Hurricane Camille. On August 19, 1969, a freak weather pattern dropped twenty-seven to thirty-one inches of rain within five hours. Camille had been downgraded to a tropical depression, but three weather patterns created a monster.

"The counter-clockwise flow of air created by the storm drew huge amounts of moisture from the Atlantic Ocean into the storm center. Then, an orthographic lifting, or updrafts of air created by the Blue Ridge Mountains, forced that moisture up into the westerly flow of air, where it was cooled to a release point, then turned into vast torrents of rain. A stalled cold front acting as a blocking force pushed the storm eastward over the mountains where the updrafts of air continued to force the moisture upward, then into even more rain."*

Damages were unparalleled. A mountainside completely caved in at Davis Creek. Many homes were demolished. Livestock drowned, and entire families lost their lives, as people sought help on their rooftops. Both agriculture and economics were affected for decades.

We fail to recognize the power of water until we see the devastation left in its path. Just six inches of flood water can sweep a person off their feet. Twelve inches can carry a car away, according to NWS.noaa.

When we pass through deep waters of difficulty or walk through the fire of adversities, God walks by our side. Trials are inevitable, but unlike the flood waters of Camille, they will never overpower us. They will never destroy us, because God walks with us.

Isaiah penned these words to Israel before God brought them out of captivity. In the preceding verse, God says, "Fear not!"

God wants us to understand that. It appears in the Bible over three hundred times. God is not only our creator and sustainer, but He is our Redeemer. We are twice bought, and we can travel through waters and fires securely for that very reason.

God wanted to remind Israel how they passed through the Red Sea. He wants us to remember there was a fourth person walking in the fire with the three Hebrews.

Let's note some specific words in our verse. It says "when" we pass through, not "if." Troubled waters await us. Fiery trials are ahead. We may be in them now, but we are not alone.

Also, note that it doesn't say we "run" through the fire. No, we walk through it. When God walks with us, we don't need to hurry because He has the entire situation under His control. We are under the protective hand of God.

Finally, notice the word "through." We pass through flood waters. We walk through the fire. We prefer to leap across the water and the flames. Leaping is quicker. Leaping is less risky, because it carries us over the dangerous torrents and the furious blaze. but God says we will go through some things. He has a purpose and a plan, but He also has our back.

Promise 4

He shall cover you with His feathers,
And under His wings you shall take refuge;
His truth shall be your shield and buckler. (Psalm 91:4)

Often, God keeps us from harm as we traverse through waters and fires, but many times, He drives danger in the opposite direction. I loved my Gatlinburg trips, nestled in the mountains. Two days before our check-in date, my husband decided he wanted to move our dates. I agreed only on one condition, that we could still get our favorite room, 266. Normally, that is next to impossible on short notice, but it happened. It was the protective hand of God, because Gatlinburg experienced record flooding on the day we would have arrived.

I love this promise because of the contrast. First, God is compared to a hen covering her chicks with outstretched feathers. When trouble arrives, her baby chicks scurry to hide under the protection of her wings. Soft, gentle wings provide an inaccessible barrier to predators. Momma hen would give her life defending her chicks. That is the tender care of our heavenly Father as He keeps us out of harm's way.

Suddenly, we are transported from the dovelike quality of God to the highly secure military terms such as shield and buckler. According to *Easton's Bible Dictionary*, the buckler is a shield large enough to cover the entire body. Perhaps the author of this Psalm had a smaller shield in mind in addition to the large buckler and that explains his use of similar terms.

Think of the multiple times an unintended delay safeguarded you from a traffic accident. We journey many rocky roads, but God prevents us from potential dangers.

Promise 5

"These things I have spoken to you, that in Me you may have peace. In the world you will have tribulation; but be of good cheer, I have overcome the world." (John 16:33)

Jesus knew His arrest, trial, and crucifixion would shatter and scatter the disciples. As He summarized His discourse, Jesus gave the disciples and every Christian three promises in the above verse.

First, Jesus promises peace. His second promise assures us that as long as we live in this world, we will encounter tribulations, but there's another promise. We can be encouraged because Jesus has overcome the world.

In the midst of every storm, we seek peace. Let the winds settle down. Forbid the waves to churn. Let our ships stop rocking.

Enter divine peace. The peace of Jesus won't make that cancer go away. Peace won't remove the bills you cannot pay. Peace won't heal that rocky relationship, nor mend your brokenness, but it keeps you steady in the storm.

The peace of Jesus stabilizes us. It calms our anxieties. It soothes our hearts and minds.

Even though we are guaranteed tribulations, we are promised peace. A peace the world cannot offer (Philippians 4:6-7).

Then, Jesus tells us to take heart. Trouble is coming, but don't allow it to bring you down. Don't allow the enemy to whisper doubt and fear in your ear. Jesus has overcome the world. Jesus was victorious over the cross, over the grave, and over Satan and his demons. This is our victory cry.

Our oppression is really our opportunity to see God work.

Each storm we pass through is another reason to pray and observe the miracles of God. What will You do this time, Lord? Watching God work is amazing, but we cannot perceive His wonders until something is broken. That's when we have a front row seat to watch the power of God move.

I don't like the promise of squalls any more than you do, but since they are unavoidable, I prefer sailing through with peace. Since I cannot prevent the howling winds, I can lift up my chin and be of good cheer. I get to watch the Master at work. What masterpiece will You unveil for us this time?

Promise 6

For we do not have a High Priest who cannot sympathize with our weaknesses, but was in all points *tempted* as we are, yet *without sin.* (Hebrews 4:15)

Have you ever found yourself in a place where you felt all alone? Like no one had been there before? Like no one could sense the depth of your hurt?

The writer of Hebrews wanted us to understand who our God is. He is not a far-off God. He is not a statue. He isn't in a grave either. He is our living risen Savior, and He knows exactly what we endure.

Jesus suffered greatly while He walked this earth. He was mocked, ridiculed, beaten, deceived, and murdered. Whatever you are dealing with today, Jesus knows how it feels.

God the Son came down to earth and lived as a Man. He stepped out of glory to save us, but He wanted to feel our pain too. Remember His physical agonies. We find in the gospel accounts where He thirsted, hungered, and grew tired. Seeing the effects of sin on people grieved Him. He probably became frustrated with His disciples when they exemplified inadequate faith. And He knows how it feels to die.

Jesus sits at the right hand of God interceding as our High Priest. He represents us to God. Not a human, temporary high priest as in the Levitical priesthood of early Israel. Those high priests were men with faults. Jesus is Deity.

He sympathizes with our weaknesses. The Greek word for "sympathize" means "to suffer along with." When you need someone who gets your pangs, call on Jesus. In our weakness, in our trouble, we go expectantly to our High Priest.

Since He is our High Priest sitting on the throne of grace, we get more than a sympathetic ear. We get grace. Undeserved favor.

Grace abides until the storm subsides.

Jesus didn't possess an internal sin nature, but externally He resisted more temptation than we will ever face. Since Jesus refused to sin, the devil placed greater temptation on Him. Sadly, we give in long before we reach that point.

Jesus never broke under pressure. He carried more burdens than we can fathom. A load so large it caused Him to sweat blood. He felt a greater weight than we can ever handle.

Rest in the comfort that Jesus Christ knows your hurts. He knows your pains. He knows all about how you feel. This is important for our next verse.

Promise 7

"Call to Me, and I will answer you, and show you great and mighty things, which you do not know." (Jeremiah 33:3)

Keep in mind all the richness of our last promise and know that the Lord wants us to ask. He wants to hear from us. He loves our times of communion with Him.

Jeremiah was in prison when God spoke to Him in this passage. He had foretold about Jerusalem being carried away captive by Babylon. The city was now under siege. Jeremiah had sounded the warning, but no one heeded his message. Now, as everything he had spoken began to unfold, Jeremiah was imprisoned for his prophecy. but God tells the weeping prophet and God tells us to call on Him.

The "mighty things" in this verse refer to inaccessible things. Things that cannot be known unless God reveals them. Where else would we go when we need guidance? The Lord is the only one who knows the correct choices for us.

These promises should convict and convince us how vital prayer is in the life of a believer. Shelter your prayer time. Increase it. Tell God about everything, big and small.

Promise 8

...Do not sorrow, for the joy of the Lord is your strength. (Nehemiah 8:10b)

Imprisoned and chained to a guard, Paul wrote several of his epistles, including the "joy epistle" Philippians. How could Paul rejoice without church-planting and preaching as he did on his missionary journeys?

Paul believed God's promise in our focal verse: the joy of the Lord is our strength. Paul lived Christ (Philippians 1:21). In the original Greek text, the verb "is" doesn't appear in the text. So, Paul lived Christ. Paul's enemies had intended his imprisonment for evil, but God had used it for good. Paul recognized that, and he rejoiced.

The enemy seeks to steal, kill, and destroy our joy. Nothing pleases him better than to see grimacing Christians. He has no authority over God's children. One of his plots involves zapping our joy. Sadly, we allow him.

We fall for his trickery, and the devil knows better than most Christians that the joy of the Lord is our strength. He steals our joy and leaves us weak.

But we are not without hope. We can turn our faces toward the Son and away from our circumstances. Away from the depression, the loneliness, the pain, the anxieties, the season we find ourselves in. We don't find joy in those places, but when we face Jesus, we see joy, for Jesus is joy.

We live in a topsy-turvy world, and sometimes life takes an even more confusing turn before we get right-side up. We allow circumstances to dictate our emotional thermometers rather than trusting our sovereign Lord. Sweet friend, we are measuring the wrong thing (topsy-turvy). God allows things, painful things, into our lives to turn us right-side up.

We can take our joy back when we live Christ as Paul did. When we commit to praise God no matter what, we will find strength through joy. When we can look at our messy lives and know Jesus loves us. When we look through joy-colored glasses, we are made strong.

Promise 9

But may the God of all grace, who called us to His eternal glory by Christ Jesus, after you have suffered a while, perfect, establish, strengthen, and settle you. (1 Peter 5:10)

This promise is for the dear saint of God who has suffered for a while. A long while. I hope that isn't you. I pray it isn't you, but if it is, I'm relieved you have found this promise today. God has you here for that purpose.

He knows you feel He has forgotten you. He knows the rhythm of your battered heart. He has collected your tears in a bottle, or a gallon jug. God has a message for you today, my friend. Hope for the momma who has all but given up on that child. Hope for that sweet sister who awakes each morning, only to be reminded her husband is no longer there. Hope for the cancer patient who just can't hear the words "cancer free." Hope for the one living in tremendous pain, physical and emotional.

God is giving you that hope today. He wants you to hold on to this promise. Memorize it. Pray it. Hold God to His promises, because He is faithful. This season of suffering will pass. Not today. Not the way you would prefer, but God loves you.

We cannot understand why we hurt, nor why we struggle for so long. We certainly don't comprehend the snowball effect while our trials enlarge as life speeds downhill. We can't understand why a good God allows pain.

But we do understand God is good. We can sing "Good Good Father" with confidence. We know truth, and this promise tucked away in Peter's first epistle is the nugget of truth you need today.

We have been called to suffer. No, Carolyn, Peter says we are called to God's eternal glory. Same thing. Our pain gives God glory.

God receives glory from your story.

Our testimonies give Satan heartburn because we refused to fall apart. OK, maybe we fell to pieces a time or two, but the master potter put us back together. Better than before.

This turmoil you find yourself in is the refining process, and you, sweet friend, will emerge as gold. That is God's perfecting work.

When I consulted with Siri for the definition of "establish," certain terms stood out: recognize, accepted, and "show truth." A day will come when you stand firmly recognized as proof of God's truth. People will know you made it, and they will be reassured they can make it too because of God's rich truth. The weakness dragging you down today is being overpowered by God's strength.

Suffering comes to make us stronger.

And settled. You will not always be tossed by the tempest, nor whipped by the whirlwind. Life will settle down.

Until our storms pass, we can trust in God's grace. We can rely on His strength. We can remind our emotions about this truth, and steady ourselves in God's promise. A promise from a good Father.

Promise 10

"No weapon formed against you shall prosper,
And every tongue which *rises against you in judgment*
You shall condemn.
This is *the heritage of the servants of the Lord,*
And their righteousness is *from Me,"*
Says the Lord. (Isaiah 54:17)

This is a fitting Scripture to close this book. The fears we fight. The doom of discouragement. The downfall of doubt, and the weariness of worry are all from the enemy. They are his weapons.

In the preceding verse, God said He created the blacksmith who manufactures weapons of war. God also created the evil men who harm others with those weapons, but in this verse, God reminds us He is sovereign. He will not allow those weapons to prosper. God has existed from everlasting to everlasting. He created all angels. God could have destroyed Lucifer and the fallen angels long ago, but He didn't. He planned to show our enemy a creature lesser than angels (mankind) who can trust in God and triumph over all demonic forces.

At times, God prevents the bullets of the enemy from striking us, the heritage of the Lord. At other times, the weapon hits its target. Whether it is disease, debt, disability, drugs, divorce, disaster, or any dilemma the enemy has thrown your way, it is his weapon. Scripture doesn't say the weapon is never formed, but that it never prospers.

When we fall under enemy fire, God allows it for a greater good.

God turns evil around for excellence.

Even when that weapon comes against us, it still never prospers because God uses it to mature us. God works it out for good (Romans 8:28).

The tongues that rise against us can range from criticism to jealousy. From slander to bitter gossip. Sharp arrows are hurled at us from the lips of others. They strike us on social media. They travel down the grapevine until they reach us.

I have allowed these wounds to fester in the past. Many times, bitterness took root, and then I had to forgive.

Forgetting now is easier than forgiving later.

As my mom used to tell me, let it go in one ear and out the other. Capture those thoughts and release them. Erase them from the hard drive of your mind. God will never allow them to harm His anointed.

My prayer is that you will never be the same after reading this book. You will never submit to your emotions, but I know that isn't realistic. We are faulty humans. If we commit to trust Christ, I know we will live abundant lives. That is what Jesus Christ has promised us.

The storms of my life occurred for my good and God's glory. But that's not all. God called an inexperienced blind woman to write. That makes those trials all the more worthwhile, because they not only matured me, they have transformed you too.

As I type these final words, I want you to know you have been prayed for by Pastor Ray and my congregation at New Life Fellowship. I will continue to pray for you. You have received eyes of faith. You have the keys to living an abundant life. You are a victor, because as Dr. Tony Evans says, you fight from a point of victory, not for victory. Prayer warrior, stand tall and walk in the authority Jesus has given you. Victory is yours.

Heavenly Father, thank You for Your Word and the instruction we find there to live in victory. We praise You for Your mighty and plentiful promises. Help us tuck them away in our hearts until we need them. In Jesus' name, Amen.

Stepping Stones

The anchor doesn't stop the storm. It stabilizes the ship until the storm passes by.

God is for us, not against us.

Our oppression is really our opportunity to see God work.

Grace abides until the storm subsides.

God receives glory from our story.

Suffering comes to make us stronger.

God turns evil around for excellence.

Forgetting now is easier than forgiving later.

- https://www.newsleader.com/story/news/history/2017/09/03/unparalleled-destruction-hurricane-camille-1969/629783001/

Read More from Carolyn

- *Incense Rising: 60 Days to Powerful Prayer*
- *Incense Rising Bible Study*
- *In the Storm*
- *Faith, Freedom, and Four Paws*—the first in the Guide Dog Tales series is coming soon
- A Mountain of Faith—Carolyn posts devotionals weekly at www.amountainoffaith.com

MEET THE AUTHOR

Carolyn regularly inspires women throughout her community at Mended Ministries, an outreach of her home church. Her years as a Bible teacher enable her to dig deep into Scripture. Yet, Carolyn delivers bite-size chunks, sprinkled with humor, easy to understand, but powerful enough to transform lives. Her heart's desire is to linger with people in prayer at events where she speaks.

Carolyn has worked with speaking coach Amy Carroll (Next Step Coaching Services), attended the Proverbs 31 She Speaks conferences, and is enrolled at the Tony Evans Training Center for theological studies.

Carolyn resides in the Blue Ridge Mountains of Virginia with her husband, Tim. She loves reading, pizza, and discovering new independence with Iva.

BOOK CAROLYN NOW

Carolyn will empower you to:

- Affirm God's fathomless love and acceptance as you draw nigh to Christ.
- Diminish anxiety and enlarge your faith in God.
- Reveal the profound value of speaking and fervently praying God's precious promises.
- Seek a victorious life as God triumphs over your tribulations.
- Replace the deceptions of your emotions with God's timeless truth.
- Exchange a defeated life for the abundant life invested in Christ.

Carolyn knows what it is to live with blindness, but she calls her disability a gift from God. She shares her stories of vulnerability and conquered fears in a vast buffet of topics suitable for retreats or conferences. She is accompanied by her beautiful guide dog, Iva, a black Lab who is adored by all.

To book Carolyn, send details to: amountainoffaith@gmail.com

Made in the USA
Columbia, SC
17 July 2019